Blood Is Thicker Than Water

A NOVEL

D1569491

Jackie Glanton, MBA

ISBN 978-1-0980-6635-2 (paperback)
ISBN 978-1-0980-6636-9 (digital)

Christian Faith Publishing, Inc.
832 Park Avenue
Meadville, PA 16335
www.christianfaithpublishing.com

Printed in the United States of America

Acknowledgements

Without God and a strong sense of faith, I am nothing! So first and foremost, I would like to raise my voice and give you praise, thanks, and all the glory! Through your love God, I have learned that all things are possible if I just have faith in you and let your will be done. You have guided and stood with me through many trials and tribulations when those who claimed to be my family and friends turned their backs and abandoned me. You removed those who would meet me with ill will, jealousy and negativity off my path and flooded me with kindness from true family and friends who have brought joy and positivity into my life. With you God in my life, I can now say to anyone who will listen, don't weep or feel sorry for me, because you almighty God has given me the power to believe in my passion and pursue my dreams. I could never have done this without the faith I have in you, my Almighty God.

Thank you, my loving husband and best friend Gene! I love you so much, babe! You are the most patient and honest person I know. I have always and continue to be inspired by your faith in God and me second, as it should be. You took time on several occasions to read early drafts, giving me advice on several chapters, keeping me focused and motivated to complete this project. You are my lifelong partner who makes both the journey and the destination worthwhile. You are as important to the completion of this book as I am. Thank you so much, my love!

Additionally, my special thanks to you Brad Fruhauff for your contributions in helping me to develop my characters realistically and authentically. What an indescribable pleasure it was to consult with you on ideas and receiving constructive critiques, suggestions, testing new ideas, and new ways of thinking. Your support was invaluable in bringing this book to life. Thank you!

1

Lisa's Manifesto

"You break that man's window, Terrance, and I'll never forgive you!" Lisa cried, keeping her voice to a loud whisper. They crouched on their hands and knees behind a trash can and an old greasy barrel of some sort. Terrance, in nothing but torn jeans and dirty old sneakers that may once have been white, a scrawny and bony boy but with a lean, noble face, smiled his big, toothy smile at her.

"You couldn't hate me if I killed your cat, Sa-sa," he teased, using the nickname that became hers when he was learning to speak, a name no one outside the family was permitted to use. "Anyway, he deserves it."

"Mr. French only told Mama about us sneaking into the movies," she objected. "We was in the wrong, weren't we?"

"He always trying to scare us and curse us out every chance he get. I don't like him."

Lisa was three years older, but Terrance had the stronger personality. They had different fathers, both white men, but while Lisa was fair, Terrance was a rich chestnut brown. Nothing in their features or gestures or manner of speaking indicated any relation between the two. No one who ever saw them together took them for siblings.

"Well, I don't like him, none, either," Lisa reasoned, "but I'm not throwing baseballs through his window."

"Stay here then. I'll do it myself."

"Don't you dare."

But Terrance had catlike reflexes and was already on his feet and silently lifting the latch on the chain-link gate.

"You hold the bat," he whispered back at her.

She watched through the space between the can and the barrel as he tiptoed through the grass toward Mr. French's house, trying to choose between what they had guessed were the kitchen window and a bedroom window. Next thing she knew, he had wound up and let the ball go as hard as he could. It flew wide of the kitchen window and hit the aluminum door with a bang like a gunshot. Terrance covered his mouth with his hands, simultaneously surprised and delighted and confused.

"Get back here!" Lisa whispered, pointlessly trying to get his attention through the gap. But it was too late. Mr. French suddenly appeared, not from inside the house, but from the side, such that he was right beside Terrance. He had just come home from work and still wore his dirty jeans and matching denim shirt. It took him all of half a second to see the ball lying a few feet from his door and Terrance standing mere feet from him for him to see what was going on, and he had grabbed the stunned boy before he could get away.

"You stupid kid, crazy boy…" Mr. French didn't know precisely what to say about his catch, so he said everything he could think of in no particular order. He yanked Terrance by the arm and brought him over to a pile of sticks he used for kindling on nights when he had a fire out back, and he squeezed the boy's arm while he looked for a good switch.

For his part, Terrance was putting up a hue and cry like he'd had his arm tore clean off. He wasn't afraid of no beating, but he wasn't about to take his medicine without putting up a fight. But Mr. French was an old lumber mill man of fifty-odd years, and Terrance was hardly eight, and the old man wrestled the child over his knee. Terrance put up enough of a struggle that Mr. French apparently decided he didn't need to expose his bare behind and instead took out his vengeance on the child's bare back.

Terrance winced and whelped and cried for Jesus to rescue him, and then Mr. French let out a stupendous roar and fell over onto his side. Terrance leapt to his feet and looked to see that his rescuer, whether sent by Jesus or the other one, was none other than his sister, Lisa, brandishing the bat like a battle ax.

"All right, Lisa!" he cheered.

"Go!" she shouted back, and he fled her angry eyes as much as Mr. French's curses.

Lisa followed close upon Terrance's heels, and to their amazement Mr. French ran after them, still holding the switch. Out the yard, down the back alley, across the street and through the next alley, they laughed as they ran, exhilarated by the enormity of their transgression. It wasn't easy to run in her overalls, but Lisa had always been naturally athletic.

They cut through a neighbor's yard by climbing the back fence and then, having bought themselves some time, using the front gate, but to their surprise Mr. French showed no more deference to another's property than they had and followed them right through and across the street and up their porch and right to the front door of their house, where they banged and cried for their mama to come help them.

Mr. French was stronger than a child but not faster, and by the time he caught up to them their mother had burst out the door and was crouching down to see what had got her baby boy so frightened.

Lisa stood aside while her mama cooed and fussed over her brother and wiped away his tears. That was the privilege of being the baby, however old. And a boy.

"Here he comes, Mama!" Lisa yelled, and they looked up to see Mr. French mounting the front steps, heaving like an enraged bull.

"What you want with here boy, Mr. French?" Mama challenged him.

"This one here," said Mr. French, indicating Terrance, "tried to break my back door with his baseball, and this one here," indicating Lisa, "done hit me with the bat! Now don't you tell me they don't deserve a whipping for that!"

"I'll tell you that and more," Mama countered. "If there's any whipping to be done, I'll thank you to let me take care of it, myself. Ain't nobody touching this boy but his own mother."

7

"Ms. Joyce, I been patient with these children long enough. If you ain't gonna teach them some respect, seems to me somebody else has got to."

He lunged for Terrance, who ran past Lisa to hide behind the rocking chair. Joyce ran past her daughter and blocked Mr. French from coming after Terrance.

"Mr. French, you best get your old black butt off of my property!" she screamed.

Then he took a swing at Lisa with the stick and caught her arm as she guarded her face. Lisa screamed, and he struck her several more times. She ducked down and put the bat over her head to defend herself. She knew that she should not have hit Mr. French, but she did not understand why this man who was not her mother or her mother's boyfriend was hitting her. Moreover, she could not understand why she was left alone to confront her angry attacker.

"Mama, help!" she cried. "Make him stop!"

But Joyce could not peel herself away from her position and risk exposing Terrance. Her face contorted into a tiger's snarl.

"Hit him back, child. You got a bat, don't you?" Joyce shouted.

"Mama, help me!"

"Don't you make me call no police, Mr. French," Mama said.

"Let's see them take the side of some raggedy children and their dopehead mother over a longstanding resident. I think I'd like to see that. You go right on ahead now, Ms. Joyce, and call who-some-ever you like."

He gave Lisa two more good smacks then dropped his stick and walked away, cursing her out as a "little white man's offspring."

When it was clear it was over and they could catch their breath, Mama wheeled about and opened her arms.

"Come here, my boy. Is you all right? Did he hurt you?"

Terrance slunk out of one hiding place and hid himself in that of his mother's warm bosom. Lisa sat with her arms across her knees, crying with her head down. She clung to herself for comfort and cried less because of the beating than because, as she now felt, she had been sacrificed to save her brother. Had she been asked to, she may have chosen the same thing, but no one had thought to ask her.

"Look like he hit Lisa worse than me," Terrance mumbled against Mama's chest. Mama pet his head and rocked him.

"Lisa be all right. Lisa always be all right," Mama said quietly. She began to lead Terrance into the house. At the door, she paused to consider her daughter.

Lisa looked up into her mother's face. She wanted to ask, *Why didn't you help me?* but couldn't get out the words. It felt wrong to have to ask.

"Can you get up?" Mama asked her. Her voice, though shaking, was gentle.

Lisa rolled to one side and pushed herself up, using the wall of the house. She looked again into her mother's face, trying to ask her question with her eyes. Mama's face was sad and almost empty, but Lisa could read there all the answer she needed. *It is how it is, girl. You learn to take it or you learn to fight.*

"Come on, T," said Mama. "Let's get you some apple juice."

She led him inside, and Lisa limped to the front of the porch and leaned against the pillar. Her arms and shoulders were sore, but she felt she would recover soon enough. Up and down the street, what people there were, went about their business, mowing their lawns, playing hopscotch and basketball, coming home from work. Didn't nobody come to help them. And why would they, when her own mother wouldn't?

It seemed like ever since Terrance was born things went this way. Anything happened that made Terrance cry, Lisa would catch the blame. Anything that Terrance wanted, Lisa went without so Mama could afford it. It is how it is.

Lisa turned around and went inside. Her mother called her into the kitchen for some juice, but she ignored her and pulled herself up the stairs to her bedroom. There, she sat down at the small table she used as a desk and opened her diary to a fresh page.

Either she's right, and I'm as good as worthless, or I'm right, and she's a horrible mama, she wrote. *I don't see how I could live with myself if she's right, and I don't have any plans to up and stop living, so it must be that I'm the one who's right.*

Okay then. Who needs them? Why should I sit around waiting for her to act like a mama to me when it's clear she don't want to? And why should I expect Terrance to be anything other than the spoiled brat she made him into?

As soon as I can, I'm getting clear of this family. From this day on, I am little more than a tenant in this home, working my way through school until I can get out of here and get a job and they don't have to worry about me hanging about reminding them that there's more people in the world than just them two.

Least, that's the way I see it.

2

The Black Perspective

In a long, dark room, garish white light wrapped a pie chart around the face of a small, balding man with pale white skin and a gray suit. He stood in front of a screen and kept repeating words like "market share" and "top of mind" and "young women, 21–35."

Around the long, wooden table sat many more balding men with white skin and suits, some dark gray, some blue, some a dark chocolate brown. Most of them sat back and nodded thoughtfully, waiting for someone to raise a question so they could chime in with the thing they'd been thinking about all meeting.

Lisa looked around and tried to understand what she was doing there with these directors and senior executives. One of the men was on the young side. Still had a full head of black hair, green-eyed, in a royal blue, trim-fitting suit with a bright orange shirt and shiny white tie. He was the Big Boss's kid—"Little Boss," she called him in her mind—and he'd only been there a little over a year. He was capable enough, but he felt the need to show everyone just how capable he was. He sat forward and wrote furiously on a note pad, trying to absorb and record it all in hopes that he could formulate just one intelligent comment.

Lisa was one of only two women at the table. Whereas she was an attractive and fair-skinned African American woman, her female colleague, Jazmin, was a straight hottie with a Middle Eastern appearance. Lisa looked mature and professional in a white skirt suit; Jazmin looked like a race car in a red blouse with black stripes along the side. Both on the young side, though Lisa was several years older, both sharply dressed, with their hair carefully styled. Both were recent promotions, women who had worked hard and, conveniently, would make an established but old agency look hip and diverse.

But woe to the man who suggested they were "diversity hires" in their presence. They had worked too hard to get where they were to be told their primary value lay in their complexions, chests, and hips. Just let a male colleague try to outperform them.

They had, perhaps unsurprisingly, sacrificed much to achieve their mid-level management positions. Neither had families, though Jazmin had a live-in boyfriend and Lisa had been married for about six years. Neither had much of a social life outside of occasional Saturday nights when they could momentarily set aside the problems of their many accounts and catch a movie or a few drinks.

But again, neither of them really belonged in this room with directors and senior-level executives watching a PowerPoint presentation on the agency's performance over the year. This meeting had been called, they knew, with them as the particular audience, and it was only slowly beginning to dawn on them why.

"So as you can see—can someone get the lights?" an older man in a navy suit started saying as the small man finished his slides, "we're struggling right now to tap two large markets: suburban women, 21–35, and urban black women, 21–35."

Suddenly everyone's heads turned to the two women sitting toward the back of the table.

You didn't have to say they were diversity hires; it was enough that everyone knew they were.

"What we're hoping, Ms. Darwish and Mrs. Drayton, is that you ladies can bring some unique perspective to the accounts targeting these populations…" said Old Navy (the older man in the navy suit).

Ms. Darwish and Mrs. Drayton—Jazmin and Lisa—exchanged looks. Looks that pleaded with the other: "Please handle this!"

Lisa Drayton finally turned to address the table.

"Thank you, sir, for your vote of confidence. I'll get my team looking into it right away, as I'm sure Jazmin will, too."

"Uh, yes, of course," said Jazmin, getting her bearings.

"I'd be curious to know if you have any initial thoughts right now," said the eager young man. Lisa could have socked him in the face right there. How could she have an opinion right now? What was he implying about her?

"Well," said Lisa, addressing the man up front, "could you first tell me which accounts you wanted me to take over?"

The room grew still. Little Boss joined everyone else in appealing to the man up front. Old Navy squirmed in his fancy suit.

A man in gray pinstripes—Lisa's boss—spoke up: "Well, uh," he began, "I mean, I—*we*—thought you might be, uh, best suited… for those accounts targeting urban, uh, audiences…"

Lisa's face grew sad, though she fought to maintain a steady, open expression. It wasn't just that this kind of thing happened all the time, it was something else. The nature of the assumptions these men had about her. Her mind scanned every recollection she could find of interactions with any of them. Had she said or done anything to make them think she was "from the Hood"? Did they actually know anything about her, or were they just assuming?

"Of course, I'm flattered that you chose me to take over those accounts, Mr. Jansen," she said, addressing Old Navy again, "but I'm afraid you gentlemen may have the wrong ideas about me. I live on a nice block in Bridgeport. I drive a Chevy Lumina, for God's sake. I listen to Brahms when I go home at night…"

"Lisa," Gray Pinstripes broke in, "we didn't mean to suggest…" he looked to Old Navy for help, but Old Navy gave a quick shake of his head to indicate he didn't want to jump in. "We didn't mean *anything*. Please don't misconstrue our actions here. I personally recommended you because I thought you were the best qualified for—"

"If Mrs. Drayton doesn't feel up to this challenge—" Old Navy began.

"I think what Lisa was saying," said Jazmin, "is that even if we had some ideas about those accounts and those demographics, we wouldn't want to speculate prior to doing our due diligence and researching them some more. I'm sure she's as prepared as I am to tackle the challenge."

It *wasn't* what Lisa was saying, but it changed the subject. She wasn't sure if she should be grateful to her white colleague or just irritated. She was both, in fact, though she probably showed her irritation more.

"I think that's a fair point," said the man in the chocolate brown suit next to Jazmin. "I move we convene so these gals can start meeting with the account managers at once."

There was general agreement that this was a good way to get out of an uncomfortable situation for everyone, and soon Lisa and Jazmin were walking down the hall to their respective offices.

"I guess we get to represent the ladies and the black and brown people now," Jazmin asked.

"It's no different than before," said Lisa, "only now it's for the clients."

"Well, I have no doubt we'll knock them on their backsides, but I could do without another meeting like that for a while."

Lisa rolled her eyes.

Jazmin continued. "They don't think twice about asking *us* to market to male audiences, but when *they* have to market to women, they all of a sudden decide they need some skirts in the room."

"Yeah, well, that's senior management for you," Lisa shrugged. "I've seen it a million times."

"Well, when we're running this place, we can make inane assumptions about *them*."

"Hah, that's right. I like the way you think, girl."

"Time to get to work then," said Jazmin. "Keep it real, sister!"

Jazmin turned off toward her office and left Lisa standing before hers.

"*Sister?*" she muttered.

Not long after lunch, she was sitting among stacks of account files. She had given her team their assignments and then sat down to learn what she could about the brands she needed to sell to urban black women, 21–35. A boutique clothing company. Shoes. A fast food fried chicken restaurant. A local musician who had just signed with a mid-sized label. It was a lot to process, but that was her process: absorb and absorb and set her brain to working on the problems. Immerse herself in a dozen different worlds and try to make sense of each of them, their desires and values.

Gray Pinstripes (his real name was Dean Trucco) had come by only moments after she'd sat down to scold her for her performance at the meeting.

"What happened back there? You looked like you'd been slapped in the face," he complained.

"Did I? I guess I was a little off balance from being in there with all the big wigs."

"I recommended you specifically for this assignment—and I recommended Jazmin based on *your* recommendation. I don't need either of you causing any trouble."

Trouble? she thought. *All I did was try to be honest.* But she said, "I didn't mean to make you look bad, Dean. I'll be all right from here on out."

"I hope so. Don't prove them right about you," he sighed.

"What does that mean?" she said, noting a tone of suggestion in his voice.

Dean obviously wished he hadn't said that then decided to come clean.

"Look, there are…people here who are skeptical you have what it takes."

"Is that so? And doesn't my work speak for itself?"

"You've got creative skills, we all know that. It's when we start talking about managing people."

"Is this why I didn't get the director position?" She had felt more than qualified, but they had said it was too far a leap for her and that she should start at manager and work toward director.

"We do have a certain progression here, but yes, it's not unrelated. I vouched for you, but…"

"But…?"

Dean bit his lip. "To be perfectly honest with you, I had my own doubts, so I ultimately sided with them."

15

Lisa's face showed her confusion and disappointment. Dean quickly added, "But I told them I thought you'd prove us all wrong. I said I was rooting for you."

"Yeah, well, thanks for telling me, I guess," Lisa said. Dean offered a weak apology and shuffled away in shame. They just couldn't help themselves from trying to keep her down.

Chocolate Brown had peeked into her office about an hour after that to try to be encouraging. "I think they're looking at you as a possible director," he said. "It took me twice as long to get half as far as you have."

"Is that right?" Lisa had remarked.

"Oh, I don't mean…it's just, you're good at this."

"Why, thank you."

It didn't matter how good she was: each new account raised the same fundamental questions. Each new problem raised the specter that she wasn't as good as she thought, that she couldn't produce the same results again, that she was just some black eye candy for prospective clients.

At length she took a break to answer some emails. Among the many client emails, intra-office communications, and offers of products and services she found an unexpected email from her husband, Paul. They texted sporadically throughout the day, but him being a lawyer, neither of them had a lot of time for socializing outside of the hour or so they were together at night before they turned in. After six years of marriage, things felt comfortable enough that they could spend some time focusing on their careers. Still, an email must be something important.

And indeed, it was. He wrote that he loved her and was proud of her recent promotion to marketing manager, and he said he wanted to make her a special dinner that night. He concluded with a poem of several stanzas, written in the earnest, elaborate style of passionate men trying to impress their ladies.

It sure got her attention. She didn't even realize she was smiling when Jazmin came in the room and asked, "What's that big smile for?"

"Oh, Jazmin, hi," Lisa said, shaking herself out of the spell. "Just an email from my husband."

"Lucky girl. I'm lucky if my boyfriend *answers* a text, much less writes one."

"Oh, he doesn't write so often, but it's nice when he does. It's just a note."

"A note? Care to share it with the class?"

"It's none of 'the class's' business, thank you very much."

"Oh, come on. I need to know someone's love life isn't a daily train wreck." Jazmin put her hands together to beg. Lisa couldn't quite understand why Jazmin was being so nosy, but she also couldn't deny some pride in having a husband that got this pretty young thing's attention.

"I don't know, it's kinda personal," she wavered. Jazmin ran around the desk to stand beside her and peek at the screen.

"What, a poem? Nobody ever wrote *me* a poem! You have to let me read it!"

"All right, if it gets you off my back. But it's just between you and me, all right?"

"Of course," Jazmin said. Then she read, "'La Géographie d'une Femme.' Wow, French! Fancy, fancy.

> "In a fitful dream through the veil of sleep
> your body stretched out before me
> like an undiscovered world.
>
> I thought I was immersed in
> an aroma like warm bread, rich and honeyed,
> that floated me on its river
> to the mouth of a deep desire.
>
> The caves of your sable eyes, sealed
> to the blind fall of night, concealing
> your soul's secret joys...and pains.
>
> Your lips swayed like roses at noontide
> casting no shadow beneath their
> blood-red beauty.

Like fountains in the piazzas of Rome,
your breasts burst with the waters
of eternal hope.

"Damn, girl, I'm getting hot and bothered over here," Jazmin interjected. "Should I stop?"
"Not on my account!" said Lisa.

"Your thighs like war, surging
forces fighting against
the tireless armies of the North.

I climbed the curve of your hips and saw
two continents joined to lock away
the Oceans of Menace, Regret, and Age.

And in the depths, your sex,
a pearly pink conch, echoing with a haunting
singular stillness, a song
Calpurnia sang to Caesar.

Complete, for now and for all time—a woman
of paralyzing beauty, unselfconscious,
receiving the traveler, a visitor,
who in the sloping fields of grass
lays his grateful head to rest.

"I may need to run to the ladies' room for some, erm, personal time," Jazmin said, handing the note back. "That man is crazy about you."
"Yeah, I know. I wish he knew how crazy I was about him, though."
"He doesn't?"
"Let's just say we're from different sides of the tracks, and he hasn't quite gotten used to the idea that a girl like me would want a guy like him."

"Tell him any girl like anyone would want a guy who wrote them something like this."

"Ha! Well, wasn't there something you came in here for?"

They got down to business talking about their boutique clothier, Elle Tracy, making sure they were on the same page about the brief and the new campaign.

"You know, I heard you specifically vouched for me with Mr. Trucco," Jazmin said as they were winding up. "I appreciate it."

"Of course," said Lisa. "We have to stick together in a place like this. Besides, you do good work."

"Thanks! We should continue this over drinks after work tonight. It'll beat staying late in the office."

Jazmin looked at her with hopeful eyes.

"That's sweet, but I try to keep my work drinking and my social drinking separate," Lisa told her. Jazmin's shoulders sagged and she excused herself to get back to work.

But when she turned to leave the doorway, she nearly collided with a skinny, dark, handsome man in sweatpants and a nylon jacket.

"Hell-o!" he said. "I sure wish I was coming to see *you*."

Jazmin grimaced and said she was just leaving, clearly trying to squeeze past the man.

"All right, all right, no harm intended," he said with his hands in the air.

Lisa was instantly exasperated. "Terrance, what are you doing here? And why are you harassing my colleague?"

"Who said anything about harassing?" he said.

"You're objectifying her."

"Nothing doing. If she work here, I know she's got to be at least as smart as you. That goes without saying. Now, whether she pretty or not, that sometimes has got to be said."

"Jazmin, this is my brother, Terrance. Terrance, Jazmin. Now, she does have work to do, so if you'll please…"

Terrance slid backward and bowed as Jazmin slipped out the door and down the hall.

"I'm glad I found you in," Terrance said as he somehow stood up straight and sat down in front of her desk in a single motion.

"You knew you'd find me in or you wouldn't come all the way up here, or are you serving a higher class of customer now?"

"Now *that* is rude. Ain't you gonna offer a brother a drink?"

Terrance leaned more than sat in the chair, one leg kicked straight out in front of him and his head nearly falling over behind him. It was an attitude he adopted when trying to appear at the pinnacle of cool and unbothered. Lisa put both her feet on the floor and leaned forward with her hands folded on her desk to demonstrate how uninterested she was in anything he had to say to her.

"Can I help you with something, or do I even need to ask what it is?"

"So that's a no on the drink then? You gotta have a bottle of Henny in here somewhere, don't you?"

He actually got up and began poking around the shelves and cupboards in her office.

"T, I got work to do."

"We ain't even seen each other in a year, probably," he said. "How come you never come to the kids' birthday parties?"

"It's never a good time, I guess. We send them gifts."

"Yeah. Well, anyway, if you got work to do, I guess I'll get down to business. I got a lead on a major, uh, investment, but I need to raise some capital, see?"

"There it is," Lisa scoffed.

"Now, hold on a minute, sis. It ain't like that. This isn't no frivolity. This is me trying to clear my debts and start fresh. Legit, even."

"Legit?"

"Uh, sure. I mean, maybe not this particular investment, but after I make my wad on it, y'know?"

He plopped back down in the chair, this time holding his head in his arm awkwardly on the armrest so he didn't need to make eye contact.

Lisa glared at him, breathing slow and heavy. The last time she'd seen him, and the time before that and the time before that going back to time immemorial, he'd hit her up for money. Money he never repaid nor ever mentioned again. She'd always accepted it as the cost of being his sister, but today felt different. Today, she'd been told that she had special experience with just this sort of thing that would make her an asset for marketing to the kind of girls Terrance went around with. She couldn't give him the money and prove them right. She couldn't.

"I can't do it, T. Not today," she said. "You've had enough from me. I ain't—I'm *not*, your bank. Maybe if I thought you were trying to hold down a real job and needed to fix your car or something, but not to buy drugs with. No, I can't do it."

Terrance sighed and rolled his head around like he'd been spun around in circles.

"You sure must hate your little brother," he said to the ceiling.

"You know it's not about that, T," Lisa complained. "No more games. Please. Just go, already."

"Yeah, all right," said Terrance. He rose, bopping a little to show he wasn't fazed. At the door he looked back and said, "I guess I can introduce myself to some of your respectable colleagues on my way out."

"What you going on about, T?" said Lisa, standing. That look in his eyes worried her. She did not want him loose in her office.

"Maybe somebody's got a job for me," Terrance smiled back. "Once they know who I am and hear my tale of woe, won't they take pity on a poor black man who just wants to buy himself some bootstraps?"

Lisa pressed her hands onto her desk. "So it's like that, is it?" she said.

Terrance shrugged. "It is what it is."

"Yeah, well it's a bunch of bull, and it's always been bull." Lisa fell back into her chair. "Look, I can't do nothing here anyway. Come on by the house some time, and I'll see what I can do."

She avoided looking at him because she knew he'd be eyeing her suspiciously, and he'd be right to. She wasn't sure yet what she planned to do; she just wanted him as far from her colleagues as possible.

"All right then," Terrance stated in a low, flat voice. "And just to show you I got your back, I'mma go call Mama right now and let her know you promised to help me out like a good big sister."

Lisa tried to control her breathing through her nose. He had to bring Mama into it, didn't he? The son of a heartless mother. "Please just go," she breathed.

"Don't worry, sis. Mama gonna be right proud of you for this. She gone be so happy you stepped up to do right by me, Sa-Sa—"

"No. Don't," she stopped him. "Don't come in here talking to me like that and then call me that. It ain't right."

Terrance's shoulders fell; he knew he'd gone too far. "Yeah. All right. I gotta bounce," he said without the least bit of bounce in his voice or his step. He disappeared down the hall.

Lisa held her hands to her forehead and breathed deeply with her eyes closed, centering herself. On a good day, Terrance showing up at her place of work would be like bringing a bomb onto a boat. On a day like it had been, it felt like he had her walking the plank too.

She grabbed the fried chicken brief and flipped through it. What the hell were they looking for here? Why did they think there was some big secret to selling to young black urban women? What did they want, something like what just happened between her and Terrance?

"Yo, chick, get yo' butt some chicken," she said and smiled as she imagined presenting the tag line to the client in front of Gray Pinstripes and Chocolate Brown. She dropped the file and grabbed her purse to freshen up in the restroom.

3

At the Doctor's

A short but well-built man approached the receptionist. She thought she recognized him, so when she smiled and greeted him, she cocked her head familiarly to the side in an unconscious gesture.

"Paul Drayton," he told her. "I have a 1:15 with Dr. Morganstein."

"Right, Mr. Drayton," she replied, finding his appointment in her calendar. "Go ahead and have a seat, and I'll let him know you're here."

Paul sat in the corner near the magazine table and dug through a stack of *Time*, *National Geographic*, *Golf Digest*, and *Good Housekeeping* to find a *Sports Illustrated*. The walls of the office were a blue gray that encouraged both calm and alertness. Paul could not have told you what pictures were hanging on the wall.

He flipped through the magazine, reading captions and headlines in between checking his watch. If Morganstein wasn't running too late, he could fit this appointment into his lunch break and not draw the wrong kind of attention to himself at work.

His mind wandered to a couple of his cases that were giving him small problems like getting paperwork filed or combing through tedious documents. Then he found himself thinking about what he would tell Lisa if the news was bad.

He'd never had bad news for her before—at least, not that seemed worth telling her. They'd met when Lisa was in her mid-twenties and they'd already had steady jobs and figured out more or less how to manage a stable life. Their marriage was an even mixture of passion, companionship, and compatible visions of the future. They hardly ever fought because they rarely had anything to fight about.

If he told her he'd secretly been to the doctor's because of recurring abdominal pain, he knew she'd be more than justified in being upset.

He could count on his hands the number of times they'd fought. One of the first had to be about the wedding. Lisa didn't want to invite her family. He couldn't understand how someone could hate her own family so much that she wouldn't even want them there on her wedding day. He didn't like half his family, but he wasn't going to *not* invite them.

"That's how family works," he told her. "You invite them to important things like birthdays, weddings, and funerals, hope they don't do anything too awful, and you deal with it."

"Nuh-uh," she said. "I'm not going to play it that way. Those people aren't coming within a mile of me on my wedding day. We'll each invite ten people we actually like and have a small ceremony and reception where we'll actually enjoy ourselves."

That arrangement, of course, was going to cause friction with *his* family. He kept after her for weeks to get her to change her mind, but she wouldn't budge; she only became more irritated with him. He finally decided it was more important that they marry than that his family was satisfied.

"I want to be with you, baby," he said. "If this is really what you want, I'll do it."

"It's what I want."

At 1:22, the receptionist called him back and led him to a small room with a couple chairs, a desk, and an exam table.

Sitting in the little room always got Paul a little nervous. Though he was always on the short side, he was tough. He'd taken a few licks in his day, and he'd given plenty back. In sports he made up for his size with speed and agility. And when he was on the police force the badge gave him almost absolute confidence. But the doctor's office put him at an unaccustomed disadvantage. What was it Jerry Seinfeld said? They make you take off your pants and wait in the little room, and after that, anyone who comes in wearing pants automatically has more authority than the guy with no pants.

It doesn't even matter if you're wearing pants, Paul thought. All the waiting dissolves the pants off you. You become desperate for any attention at all.

Paul didn't do desperate well.

Footsteps approached the door and paused. Paul checked his watch—1:30. He waited for the little quick knocks that doctors give before they enter, but they were a long time coming.

If Paul had been nervous from just being there before, he felt like he had good reason now. He'd been seeing Dr. Morganstein since he was eight. They weren't exactly buddies, but he would have invited Morganstein to his wedding if he could have. As a healthy man, he mostly only got good news or confirmation of the mild illnesses he came in suspecting he had. He never knew Morganstein to hesitate.

At last the knocks came, and Dr. Morganstein swept into the office.

"Hey, Paul, good to see you!" He beamed and held out his hand.

Paul stood and shook his hand. "Hi, Doctor, how's it going?"

"Fine, fine," the doctor said as they took their seats. He gave Paul a playfully scolding look and added, "And how many times do I have to tell you to call me 'Joe'?"

"I can't get used to it!" Paul laughed.

"You will, you will," Joe Morganstein chuckled. "How's work? How's Lisa?"

"All good. You know."

"You make partner yet?"

"Uh, no, not yet. That's probably still a few years out. I have a pretty big case now, though, that'll be a big stepping stone."

"Excellent, excellent!"

Morganstein was sitting forward in his chair with disconcerting intensity. "Lisa was hoping for a promotion, too, last time we talked, wasn't she?" he said.

"Well, yeah… It ended up going to someone else…"

"Oh no," said the doctor. "That's a shame."

"But she got a different position. A good one, though not the one she wanted. She's got her own big client, too, that could change things for her."

"Oh, well, that's great then."

Paul waited for Dr. Morganstein to get down to business, but the good doctor just sort of sat there smiling at him with a faraway look in his eye.

"So, uh, Doctor—"

"'Joe,' please," Morganstein interjected. "One of these days you'll get used to it," he added with, Paul thought, a forced chuckle.

"Uh…*Joe*, what's going on? It feels like you're stalling."

Joe Morganstein's warm smile demurred into a grimace as he sat back in his chair.

"Yes, I suppose I am," he admitted. "Look, Paul, does Lisa know you're here?"

"Why do you ask?"

"Because I need to talk to you about something, and it's going to be important for you to talk with her about it."

"What is it?"

"You've always been a tough kid, Paul. I get it. Your neighborhood was rough, growing up. But you can't just barrel through some things. You need to let Lisa in on this."

"On what? Seriously, Doctor, what is it?"

"The ultrasound showed cysts on your kidneys. That's what's causing your abdominal pain."

"Okay…"

"Now, we can manage the pain with aspirin and by draining the cysts…"

"But?"

"But it's more serious than just the pain. We found more than three cysts on each kidney ranging in size from about half an inch to three-quarters of an inch."

"Meaning?"

"Meaning you have a condition called autosomal dominant polycystic kidney disease or ADPKD. It starts with pain, but it generally leads to kidney failure."

Paul stood up. His face had long since drained of its color. Imagine a lion one day discovering it was really a mouse. His whole world was rocked.

"What does this mean? We can beat this. I'll change my diet. Are there medications? Exercises? What do we do?"

Dr. Morganstein leaned forward again.

"Yes, of course, we'll do all that right away. But I also want to start screening your family for potential donor matches."

"So soon?"

"ADPKD is a genetic condition. If any of your family members is a match but has the genetic mutation for it, they won't be able to donate, and if that's the case, we'll need to get you on a donor list right away."

Paul had to sit back down.

"I can't believe this," he said and dropped his head into his hands. "Could I die from this?"

"Well, I don't want to say there's no chance of that. Kidney failure can be treated and managed in a few ways that can be pretty inconvenient but still allow you to have a pretty normal life. In some cases, though, it is possible to develop other complications that can be fatal. That's why, given your age and otherwise good health, I think you'd be a good candidate for a transplant."

"Oh my goodness. Oh my goodness."

Morganstein hung his head and gave Paul a minute to himself. The room had closed in on him and time had stopped.

He was seven again, watching from the hallway as his parents fought in the kitchen. They were cursing each other out and accusing each other of all sorts of hateful things. They couldn't see him in the shadows, but they weren't exactly trying not to wake him and his sister.

His father said something accusatory about "you and my brother," when suddenly his mother curled her hand into a fist and swung it against his father's face. Paul couldn't tell exactly what happened. His father was caught off guard and fell sideways into a cabinet, but it was like he bounced off of it and there was a flash and then his mother was on the ground and his father was standing over her with his fist balled and it seemed to Paul that it was smoking like the barrel of a gun.

His mother lay there crying, and his father all of a sudden realized what he'd done and backed away in horror. His father walked out the back door. His mother slowly picked herself up, grabbed her purse, and left out the front door. A car door opening, closing. An engine creaking to life, revving, and fading as it moved away into the night.

Paul crept into his sister's room and looked out her window. Out on the lawn, his father leaned with his arm against a tree like a marathoner trying to catch his breath. The moon was full and bright and accusing.

That was the first time the world had ended for Paul. He felt cast adrift, alone. He didn't know what to do or where to turn. He heard the rustle of sheets and saw that Ashley was sitting up in bed with the sheets pulled up around her, had probably been sitting there listening to the fight like he had. He sat down beside her and put his arms around her. This much he knew was right to do.

In the morning, their father found them still wrapped in each other's arms, asleep in an improbable pile on Ashley's bed. They didn't see their mother for three days.

"Paul? Paul?"

Dr. Morganstein's gentle voice called Paul back to the present.

"Paul, there might be…another option."

There was already so much to process he didn't pick up on Morganstein's tone.

"What do you mean?"

"There are…ways…to sort of 'fast track' a transplant. I don't like to do it—I've never done it, in fact—but you were a good cop, and you're a good defense attorney…"

"I'm not…I don't understand."

"You've served this city well, and you've been a good…friend… to me, so I could see my way to…pursuing…this other option."

Paul held his head in his hands and tried to think it all through. Something was clearly off.

"It's not legal. That's what you're saying," he finally said.

"Well…let's say it's a gray area, a matter of my discretion as a physician. But yes, I could get in some trouble."

"Jail time?"

Morganstein inhaled. "Yes."

"Out of the question."

"You don't have to decide now. I appreciate your integrity. I do. That's precisely why I'm willing to do this. Just think it over."

"I don't need to think it over. What's the next step?"

Joe talked him through several forms of medication and dietary recommendations to manage his symptoms and improve his prognosis.

"And there's one more thing," he concluded. "You need to tell Lisa."

Paul sighed almost as heavily as when he'd heard the diagnosis.

"I suppose I do. She gets so worried, though."

"You can't protect her from this forever, Paul. We're talking about surgery here. Possibly medication for the rest of your life."

"Yeah."

"You'll need her support."

Paul squirmed in his seat.

"She needs *my* support," he said as if to himself.

"Well, support each other then," said Morganstein. "That's marriage."

"Yeah…marriage. Thanks, Doctor."

"Joe."

"Joe."

4

Black Mirror

The Orange Line was quiet as she rode home late that night. In the dark, the L car was like a capsule of light racing above the busy city streets. But that light, a pale blue light that was neither bright nor warm, offered little comfort. It only seemed to amplify the feeling of the dark as it turned the windows into black mirrors for the passengers to watch each other in.

Bridgeport was becoming an increasingly diverse middle-class neighborhood, and the passengers reflected it. Several white professionals of Polish and Italian extraction. An Asian-American youth in a jogging suit and wearing large headphones. An elderly woman speaking in what was probably Russian to the elderly man beside her. An African American female professional in a white skirt suit.

Lisa watched the Asian-American boy at the other end of the row via the window's reflection. It seemed like ages since she'd been that young, though she'd only really been out of college for less than ten years.

Days like today were exhausting in every way. At the best of times, she liked her job; marketing was exciting. Coming up with ways to present a product to customers on TV or billboards or the radio. Looking for that emotional hook that drew someone in and made them say, *Yeah, I want to feel like* that!

But you couldn't get any of the excitement without the constant scrutiny and pressure to live up (or down) to expectations. Hardly a day passed without a co-worker commenting about or asking her something, the subtext of which was, "You're black, you must know about this," or what was worse, "You're a woman: can you handle this?"

It could be lonely too. Most folks saw one another as competition for the better positions—even when they weren't any good at the job they were already supposed to be doing. Gray Pinstripes was a decent boss, but he couldn't see past the job itself. People weren't people to him; they were roles that they played with greater or lesser skill and talent. There were few other women, and only one other brother, but she stayed away from him. Everyone was so eager to introduce them to one another her first day, but that only made them both want to avoid each other after that. What, because they were both black they were supposed to be best friends at work?

College taught her that white folks were well meaning, just dumb. It was rare you got a taste of real, aggressive prejudice or discrimination. Most of the time it was just unexamined assumptions, ideas about black folk they picked up from the air or their mother's milk. A gentle correction here or there could solve most misunderstandings without them even noticing they'd been offensive.

Mama never prepared me for the white world, she thought. Maybe she thought there were enough white folks at school, though they were a virtual minority. But then, why was she even thinking about Mama? Her mama never taught her much except that she was ugly and skinny and didn't know how to catch the boys' eyes. Or that she wasn't a good kid like her little brother, Terrance. Her little brother who'd been picked up by cops four times before he was sixteen and had spent nearly one hundred days in jail before he was twenty-one. Nothing and nobody was ever good enough for Mama—except T. Even with her fancy job in a fancy office in a fancy building almost downtown, she wouldn't ever be good enough for Mama.

'Course she'd have to tell Mama something first in order for her to say something critical and dismissive about it, but Lisa was done giving her the satisfaction of tearing down her daughter every chance she got. Terrance knew that even the mention of Mama was painful to her, and that's why he'd said it. He wasn't a bad man; he just never got on his feet long enough to show people how good he could be. What was a couple hundred dollars here or there between siblings? Or as a gift from a sister to her younger brother.

But don't make this about Mama. If Mama wanted to have a relationship with her, she knew how to reach her. It must have been almost five years since they last spoke, and it hadn't been pretty.

Mama had never trusted Paul. Paul who had hardly spoken seven unkind words to her since she'd known him. Paul who had helped her pay for her last few college courses.

You can't trust no cop, her mama had said. *Especially no white cop. You damn sure can't marry one! Ain't you got a lick of pride in your people?*

Lisa defended her husband, but Mama would have none of it, even suggesting Paul already had some white girl on the side. Lisa told her to stop comparing Paul to one of her own sorry looser boyfriends. Mama slapped her across the face and bawled her out really good, but there were tears in her eyes. Lisa had gone too far. It was a family trait, hurting one another. Mama marched off cursing her, and they hadn't spoken since.

The irony, of course, was that both Lisa's and Terrance's fathers were white men, white men her mother had trusted but who, to her mind, had betrayed her. Ever since Mr. French beat her, Lisa had begun to wonder if her mother hadn't done something to run those men off. She'd had many good white friends, and now Paul, who had become her rock.

She hadn't spoken with her mother since then—not in reality anyway. They'd had many conversations, or rather, arguments, in Lisa's mind. The hard truth of the matter was Joyce's voice was never far from Lisa's consciousness. It haunted her like an accusing conscience. It terrorized her like a poltergeist.

It was there in the conference room when Old Navy and Gray Pinstripes and dumb Little Boss gave her urban black women, 21–35.

Ooooh, look at that now. What all those white mens looking at you for? You thought you was sharp stuff around here, but end of the day you still just a ghetto-little black nothing to them. I told you so. I told you so.

It's a misunderstanding, Mama. It ain't no thing.

White folks ain't innerested in understanding, baby. Go on and tell 'em. Tell 'em where you from. Tell 'em 'bout your poor mama working her butt off ever day for you and your brother. Tell 'em 'bout Terrance working the streets. They already assume them things is true about you, anyways.

That ain't me, Mama. That *isn't* me. I'm college educated. I read books. I have a career. That isn't me, and I'll show them all.

Lisa laid her head against the window. It was too late at night to worry about her hair anymore, and she had an appointment at the beauty shop the next day anyway. She tried to see through her reflection in the window to make out the tiled pagoda roofs of Chinatown. She wondered if the Asian-looking boy would get off soon. She wondered if her bosses really knew anything about her or were making assumptions—just as she herself was making assumptions. She wondered if she really did have a unique perspective on urban black women, 21–35.

Look at you, Ms. Career Woman, thinking you're all that because you squeeze your fat butt into a little skirt and wave it around for some old white men who tell you what to do.

Yeah, well, at least I'm not so skinny anymore.

You think you better than your own family 'cause you take the train downtown ever day and leave us all behind? You making all that money, but you still a ghetto-little black nothing from the hood.

No, Mama, not anymore. That is all in the past.

What kind of wife are you? Working to all hours of the night, leaving your man at home to cook his own dinner while you drink gin with rich white boys.

Lisa scoffed out loud at the image of her drinking gin with her boss. No one took any notice. But the thought of Paul and dinner got her worried. She hadn't even *thought* to call him and tell him she'd be late. She thought about the cell phone in her purse, but she didn't like using it, and it was borrowing trouble to call now. She'd have to fight with him over the phone *and* when she got home. Better to leave it for now.

The Asian-American boy got off at the next stop and a young white couple with holes in their jeans and all sorts of chains and spikes on their bodies sat down in his place.

Good luck, kids, Lisa thought. *You think you're expressing yourself, but it's never as easy as poking a hole in your body. They'll find a way to drag you down. Ain't no freedom but in death, I suppose.*

Of course, she loved and respected Paul, but something about the responsibility, even after six years, weighed on her, choked her like one of those kids' chains pulled too tight around her neck. Every day of her life since she could remember there was someone wanting something from her, expecting something whether she wanted to give it or not.

That's life, kids. You'll find it out soon enough. One or the other of you will start wanting something from the other one, and you'll be like, "What the freak?" but there won't be nothing you can do about it.

She'd met Paul when she was still living at home and he was a cop working patrol in the neighborhood. She had been working as an administrative assistant and taking night courses to finish her undergraduate degree, so it was rare she was even hanging out on the porch or anywhere he might run into her. Somehow, he must have spotted her, though, and then he suddenly had to check in often at the library where she often studied.

Like anyone from the hood, she tried to steer clear of the police for any reason. As a woman bettering herself through education, however, she wanted to believe she was becoming more open-minded. So when he strolled into the library, hung around the stacks near her table, and finally came up to talk to her, she played it cool, like she spoke with gun-toting members of the white power structure all the time.

She had to admit he was cute, the way he seemed more afraid of her than she was of him, the way he tried so hard to find things to talk about. In a funny way, his attentions proved to her that she was succeeding at reshaping herself, that the path she had chosen to leave home and become something was no mere fantasy, that the world outside recognized what she was doing.

Then it was her stop. She exited the car into the pale orange glow of the city. The sky was clear, but she could only make out a couple stars. All the stars in this city came from the towers of glittering yellow windows in the distance and the rivers of red and white lights flowing around them. The neighborhood to the south was dark and dim by comparison.

She went to the stairs and descended from the platform onto the cracked sidewalk below. The people wandering around Bridgeport at that time of night did not, generally speaking, wear white skirt suits and carry designer purses. They were younger, often ethnically Asian or European, and on their way home from work or out to a bar or show or coffee shop. She kept her car in a lot half a block from the stop. Generally, she felt safe but still walked briskly to avoid tempting fate. Tonight, she could not choose between rushing to get home sooner or dawdling to avoid the fallout of her negligence.

It is what it is. That's what we tell ourselves, she thought. *But we always mean, "It sucks, deal with it."*

She found her car and drove away toward home.

5

Meet the Draytons

Lisa drove a nice car and lived in a nice house in a nice neighborhood. It was nice, but not too nice. It was the kind of neighborhood with quaint, black streetlights meant to look like old gas lamps, where you could hear dogs barking at any time of day, where kids played soccer in the street or threw a football back and forth. It was the kind of neighborhood where everyone owned the home they lived in and spent the weekend mowing the lawn and trimming the hedges.

It was the kind of neighborhood where people *had* hedges. And it was the kind of neighborhood where people could almost believe it was nicer than it was.

Her car clearly had a white exterior, but it showed gray in the shadow of night. When she had parked on the street and stepped out to walk up to the house, her white skirt suit had the same gray appearance as the car. Below that a satin blouse of some fuchsia or rose color caught the porch light. With only the stars to help her, she tried to make out the time on her wristwatch. She failed, but it didn't seem to matter. She huffed in frustration and glanced at the house with a mixture of concern and discouragement.

Her heels clip-clopped on her way to the front door. When she reached it, she paused a moment before turning the knob. Had someone been watching, they might have seen, even by the weak light over the door, that she was beautiful, with high cheekbones but round cheeks, deep, intelligent eyes, and a straight, simple nose. It was the kind of face that could hardly look other than lovely, whatever the lighting, whatever her makeup, whatever her mood.

This night, it was lovely still though her forehead creased and her mouth twisted with worry. At last she put on a smile and burst into the house with a jangle of the brass knocker.

"Hi, honey!" she called out. She flipped on the foyer light, locked the door behind her, dropped her purse down by the door, and disentangled her feet from her strappy shoes, all the while shouting down the hall in a rushed voice. "I'm sorry I'm late again! You should see the mound of work on my desk. It's a little embarrassing. I've been taking meetings in the conference room just so no one has to see it. Then I got to the platform just as the train was leaving and had to wait for*ever* for the next one. Smells like you made something nice for dinner, though! I haven't eaten since dinner last night, I think, other than a protein bar and an apple. I may be *literally* dying of hunger. Oh, wow, you really went all out here!"

She had stepped into the dining room and discovered her husband sitting at a table laid out in style: red candles, half burnt down in their silver candlesticks; the nice china, silverware and napkins precisely placed; a fresh garden salad with yellow-gold peppers and glistening wedges of tomato; a dark merlot poured into goblets; and in the center of it all a thick lasagna—his mother's recipe—its cheese toasted at the edges and in little mounds across the surface, promising that exquisite, sensual mix of brittle and chewy.

Except the lasagna had long since stopped steaming, and the shine of the cheese had dulled into a cloudy whiteness, and the juice of the tomatoes had leaked all over the lettuce. How long had he spent preparing this meal? How long had he sat waiting for her?

"And I didn't even call!" she said. "Paul, baby, I'm so sorry."

Her husband, though ten years older than her, was still not old. A couple years of making a name for himself as a newly minted lawyer had put some gray in his short brown hair and even in his finely trimmed goatee.

"You said you'd be home early today" was all he said, and he said it quietly, but she felt as if he'd shouted it straight into her heart.

"I did, I did, but I got thrown these new accounts and I wanted to get everything started with them. They could be really important for me. I really am sorry, hon, this looks—"

Before she could finish—he knew what she was trying to say, anyway—Paul growled and with a furious gesture swiped his place setting off the table. The goblet of wine spilled too, and the purple-red liquid flowed onto the butter dish and soaked immediately into the creamy white table linens.

"Paul, what the hell?" the woman shouted, more surprised than upset. She noticed that the wine bottle was at least half empty and Paul had been drinking from his glass.

"Forget it. I'm going to McGrady's," he said.

"What do you mean, 'you're going to McGrady's'?" You just broke our china plate! What's the matter with you?"

"With me? With *me*? What's the matter with *you*? You know what? Forget it. Just forget it." He tried to walk past her, but she set herself on both feet before him and put her hand to his chest to stop him. He was not much taller than her, but he was much stronger, and he could have bowled her over, but he only pushed enough to let her feel his strength.

"I'm not gonna *forget* anything," she snapped. "Now, I *said* I'm *sorry*."

"Yeah, you always do, don't you?" he scoffed. "But then it's the same old stuff happening again and again. Whatever! Do what you like."

"It's a ring, not a leash, you fool," she said, waving her left hand in his face.

"Oh, you're still wearing that thing?" he shot back. "I thought you had all these important things going on."

"I do. It's called my *career*."

"Well, there's a microwave in the kitchen. You can go have dinner with your career."

Now he pushed into her and knocked her back a couple steps. This she could not tolerate. He tried to pass her, but she grabbed his arm. He flung it off. They stared each other down with faces just daring one another to do something they'd regret. He flinched his shoulders at her as if he might spring, but she kinked her chin back at him and he didn't move.

She wasn't sure if she should be afraid; it wasn't their first spat. But she couldn't let anyone talk to her like that. She would never let anyone talk to her like that.

Paul seemed to consider his options and decide against most of them. He turned away from her.

"I'm going to McGrady's," he murmured.

But she wasn't done fighting, so she took one last jab: "Maybe you'd better, and maybe you'd best not come back, 'cause if you want to do me like that it is not going to go well for you in *this* house!"

He stopped and stood in the middle of the foyer.

"'Do you' like *what*, exactly?"

"Like...like..."

"You can't even say it," he said, shaking his head. He slowly turned to face her again. Her face suddenly became frightened, her body tense.

"Look, baby," he started, "I know I'm rough around the edges, but I'm *nothing* like—"

"Paul..." she warned.

"Like your mother's boyfriends," he continued, "or—"

"Paul, you shut up now!"

"Or your *brother*," he finished.

"You ignorant fool," she said and began to slap him repeatedly. He caught her wrists and she struggled for a moment, but the fight was dying out of her; she was just hurt. "Okay, you win. You happy now?"

"Happy? 'Cause I gotta hurt you to get your attention? No, I'm not 'happy.' I *love* you, Lisa. I just want to feel like part of your life sometimes is all."

"Oh, honey," she gasped. "What have I done? I'm messing everything up."

She sat down on a stair and held her face in her hands. He sat beside her and put an arm around her.

They sat in silence for some time while she cried.

"What was the occasion?" she asked, nodding toward the dining room.

"Big new client. Big bonus," he shrugged.

"Baby, that's wonderful," she cooed. She leaned into him and pressed her head into his shoulder. His arms began to enfold her as if impulsively, inevitably. She looked into his eyes, and he returned her needful gaze. The time for apologies was past, and now they were only aware of their desperate longing for each other.

Soon they were kissing. Rough, sloppy kisses like couples can only give when shielded by the privacy of their intimacy. Moments later, the white blazer was on the floor and the zipper to the matching skirt was open and the buttons to the fuchsia-rose blouse were being pulled from their holes and the sloppy, rough kissing was hard to maintain as they ascended the stairs but they did it anyway and it was dark in the bedroom and their breathing was heavy and her face was lovely and made pale by the moonlight as he lowered her into the bed.

A bedside lamp clicked on and lit a sphere of yellow in the corner of the room. Her skirt and blouse lay on the floor. Close by were Paul's Dockers and a green polo shirt, and inside these a white undershirt and a pair of briefs, as if parts of the outer garments. Paul, still in his black wool business socks, stood up beside the bed, extricated the briefs, and pulled them on.

In the bed, Lisa, intractably lovely, had the sheets pulled up to her chin as she watched him. Her eyes still glowed with her passion and reached out to him as if trying to hold onto him.

Their lovemaking had been of that desperate sort when lovers cannot find the words to fix the mess they've made of things—needy, impulsive, physical almost to the point of violence. As much for their own release as for restoring their connection with one another. Now that it was over, there was no more need for talking or fighting.

"I'll go clean up the dining room," Paul said in a tone as matter-of-fact as the briefs and socks he walked away in.

Paul was no-nonsense like that. Had she just called, he would have felt she'd done right by him, and he'd have packed up the dinner he'd worked so long to prepare without a second thought. Now that their fight was over, he would do the same.

Before getting out of the covers, Lisa shimmied back into her panties. Only then did she rise, and holding one arm across her breasts, find a cotton-knit nightgown in her dresser and take it into the bathroom, closing the door behind her.

Lisa, in contrast to her husband, was capable of a certain amount of nonsense. She had learned much of it growing up in a home that never let her forget people were watching her, but still she'd turned herself into a successful woman who, she knew, had nothing to be ashamed of.

Once the door was closed, she dropped her nightgown on the floor and stood before the mirror in reflexive self-assessment. In the bright light of the vanity and against the white tiles of the shower behind her, her skin seemed to grow three shades darker. The same happened when she stood at the locker room mirrors with her pale-skinned white friend, Mila.

On her best days, Lisa knew she was beautiful, but perhaps because she and Paul had fought, this night she couldn't help but feel self-conscious. Her beauty was of that curvaceous variety typically more valued among her black friends than her white ones. Her curves and her dark eyes and dark hair all practically shouted, "Here comes a black woman!" yet in that same locker room mirror, beside her black friends like Shelly and Chassidy, or especially Veronica, she looked pale as an onion.

Mila would say, "The things I'd do for boobs and hips like yours!" while Lisa would think, *You should talk, with that gorgeous auburn hair.* Or Shelly would say, "You always have such good hair," and Lisa would think, *What do you have to complain about with that beautiful bronze skin of yours?*

Once Veronica said much the same thing, something along the lines of "I wish I was lighter like you, Shelly." Lisa pounced on it. "Don't you say it, girl. You know you beautiful the way you are."

"Oh, Lisa, calm down," Veronica said and rolled her eyes. "I'm just saying it's hard to get guys to notice me when they think it's unlucky if I cross they path."

Lisa smiled with the memory but scrunched her face in frustration at herself and all womankind. She hated this kind of fussiness over appearance, even if she enjoyed making herself up pretty. *Why do I care so much? I'm pretty, I'm successful, I have a great husband. What does it matter?*

Of course, it mattered to Old Navy and Gray Pinstripes. She wondered what they would think if they knew how many times she'd been accused of not being "black enough" as a child.

Or paradoxically, "too black." Her mama always hated when she wore her hair natural or did her nails too long. She never knew if she did it because she liked it or to piss off her mama.

She took to scrutinizing her face for wrinkles and her hair for signs of early graying. Of course she found something to displease her; it was more or less the point of the exercise. Then she stepped back and considered her hips and butt. Just like yesterday, they looked fleshier than the day before. She lifted her breasts up to where she remembered them once being then let them drop back to resting—a little "test" that always made her laugh as her body jiggled.

Eventually she put on her nightgown and got down to her normal bedtime preparations of removing her makeup and plucking her eyelashes and putting on her creams and lotions. When she had finished and came out of the bathroom, Paul was just returning from cleaning up after their failed dinner.

He was about to get ready for bed too, but she blocked his way and made him hug her, first. Staying in his arms, she pulled back a little to look in his face then asked, "You really love me no matter what, don't you?"

Paul smirked but indulged her. "Yep. You always ask, and I always say the same thing."

It was true, but it always made her smile nonetheless.

"I'm not 'too black' for you?" she teased.

"I'm not 'too white'?" he returned. He never cared for this way of speaking, but he would usually play along rather than make a fuss.

She leaned back slightly and compared her light tan skin to his pale pink skin, the dark hair of her arms against the graying brown hair of his chest. She held her hand against his cheek and noticed again how her palms had some pink in them.

This is my man, and I'm his woman. Sure we get some strange looks sometimes; not that often, really. But we belong together, and nobody can change that.

But she knew if it bothered anyone, it was Paul, who really did feel "too white" for her, and a few minutes later, when they both got into bed and turned out the lights, she laid her arm on his shoulder and compared them again in the refracted light of the moon.

6

Conversations

Brunch with the girls was always at the Sunnyside Cafe across from the movie theater and kitty corner to an old Baptist church. The "girls" were Mila and Veronica, an unbreakable trio since high school, when they had found each other because they needed each other. You wouldn't peg them as friends if you saw them nowadays. Lisa dressed nicer and generally looked more elegant than her friends, who both worked at the same beauty parlor. Mila was a pale white girl with freckles and frizzy red hair. Veronica was a deep, espresso black with her hair pulled back so it puffed out behind her wrap.

Mila and Veronica had arrived first and spotted Lisa crossing the street, shuffling carefully in her extra-high heels. They called to her and waved, and she waved back.

"Girl, you're late *again*!" Mila said when Lisa had come through the restaurant. They all stood and exchanged hugs and kisses on the cheek.

They took their seats. They always saved Lisa a seat with her back to the church because she couldn't help herself from mocking the congregants when they left the service.

"Hey, I texted you!" Lisa protested.

"Did you really? I always forget I have that thing."

"It must have been important to be late for Sunday morning mimosas," Veronica said.

"Well, Paul and I had a little lie-in this morning," Lisa explained. Her friends ooh-ed and laughed.

"Well, all right then, girlfriend!" said Veronica.

"I say it's about time," Mila added.

"You would," said Lisa.

"Damn straight. I gotta look out for my girls."

"Yeah, well, I can look out for myself just fine when it comes to my husband. So what were you girls talking about before I got here?"

"You, of course," Veronica said.

"There are worse subjects, I'll tell you that much," Lisa said, waving her off.

"Well, you might think different when you know what we were saying," Veronica said. "Yolanda been talking down at the beauty shop that your brother been edgy lately. She worried he gonna go off for good one time."

"Not this," said Lisa. "He just came by my office on Friday. I thought he was gonna get me fired."

"Yolanda's saying something's different this time," said Mila. "Like, he's acting like nothing's wrong, but she can tell he's jittery and scared."

"Can we talk about something else?" Lisa said.

"We thought you'd be worried 'bout Yolanda and the kids," said Veronica.

Lisa covered her face with her hands and sighed. "Ladies, truth be told, I'm feeling the pressure, lately. I got a big thing at work, and I been neglecting Paul, and this thing with Terrance now just feels like too much."

"Oh, honey," her friends replied, and Mila leaned over and gave Lisa a hug, getting her curly read hair in her face.

"What's going on with Paul?" Mila asked after a moment.

"Oh, I don't want to get into details."

"C'mon, Lisa," Veronica complained. "You never get into details."

"And I'm not going to start now."

The waitress brought a round of mimosas for them and they sipped the sun-gold liquid and watched the people passing on the street. A burly man in a puffy coat and cargo shorts was walking a teacup yorkie. A huge woman with a flowery dress and an expansive hat labored past, each step an effort. Several young couples pushed children in strollers.

"Yolanda says your mama been sick," Veronica suddenly said to Lisa.

"Oh, yeah?" Lisa said without taking her eyes off the crowds.

"I just thought maybe you'd heard."

"No, I hadn't."

Mila and Veronica exchanged knowing, exasperated looks.

Mila said, "Lisa, she's getting old. You should at least check in on her."

"And you should mind your own business."

"You're in a mood today, or something," said Mila.

"I'm just tired of people telling me about my mother is all."

"Who people? We're just worried about you."

"And you should talk," Lisa said, scowling at Mila. "When was the last time you 'checked in' on your mother?"

"That's not fair," Mila complained. "You know what she did to me."

"And you know what my mama did to me!"

"She was always so nice to me, bad as she was to you. And now she's sick with who-knows-what."

"Yolanda says it's just a cold or something," Veronica offered.

"See?" said Lisa. "Nothing to worry about. Don't you have somebody else's beauty shop gossip we can talk about?" she asked Veronica.

"Well, did you hear about Missy?" Veronica said, growing serious and leaning in close.

"What about her?"

"Nobody seen her for a few days now," Veronica continued. "Say she's taken the kids and gone to live with her mama for a while."

"Why?" Mila asked. "I thought she had some new man."

"Yeah, so did everyone one else, but no one's seen him yet."

"You think he's sneaking around with her?" Lisa asked.

"No one's really sure, but Carmen saw some dude go into her house the other night carrying a bat—"

"A *bat*?" Lisa asked. "Like, a baseball bat?"

"Well, yeah, I assume he didn't mean no flying rat thing. She said a *bat*. Well, she watched a few minutes more, being worried something was going to go down. Then she heard screaming and a gunshot."

"What?" Mila said.

"But it wasn't her, right?" said Lisa. "If she's gone to her mama's?"

"Maybe wasn't anybody," said Veronica. "Carmen didn't know what to do, so she tried calling. No answer. Then after a few minutes she went over there, and she couldn't hear or see nobody in the house."

"Oh my goodness," said Lisa.

"Well, what? Did he kidnap them or something?" said Mila.

"Carmen says Missy called her the next day and said she'd be out of town but that she was all right."

"I hope so."

Lisa hesitantly asked, "Does anyone know who the man was?"

"Carmen didn't get a good look at him, but she thought she recognized something in his shape and walk."

"You mean like it's somebody we know," Mila said.

"I'm only saying what I heard from Carmen," Veronica said, holding her hands up defensively. "But yeah, it sound like it."

The women grew silent again. It was an all too common kind of gossip, but they never took any real joy in it. But for the grace of God it could have been them many a time.

They polished off their mimosas and ordered another round. Veronica said what someone always said after telling or hearing such a story: "Well, it is what it is. We shall see."

The church bells rang to indicate the end of the service, and people began to file out wearing their suits and dresses.

"Sometimes it feels like there's just no good news," Lisa remarked. "Speaking of which, how's your new man, V?"

"What new man?" she scoffed. "The 'Ghost of Pine Street'?"

"Are you serious? What'd you have, like two dates?"

"Not even. He disappeared mysteriously on his way to meet me for date number two, best I can tell. Nobody's seen *him* none either—and no," she added, turning to Mila, "he ain't Missy's man neither. Missy's man was sort of medium and athletic, not long and tall."

"You just can't catch a break," Mila said.

"Can't everybody find a man like Paul," Veronica said, thinking she was joking, but Lisa let out an involuntary grunt.

"Now what's that mean?" Mila asked.

"Ah, nothing, I shouldn't have said anything."

"Nuh-uh," said Mila. "You don't get to shrug us off. Tell us what's wrong."

"We talked enough about me already."

"Guess it's your morning to have all the problems," said Veronica. "You get a turn once in a while—when Mila's having a slow week."

"Ha-ha," said Mila. "Now, lady, you just said you and Paul were doing good this morning, then you tell us you're messing things up, and now you're grunting about what kind of man he is. I think you owe us an explanation. What's going on?"

They sipped in silence some more. Her two friends could see she was struggling to put something into words. A motorcycle sped past, the engine noise rattling off the buildings for blocks.

"Something happened a couple nights ago that shook me up a bit is all," Lisa began.

"With *Paul?*" Veronica said.

"Did he put his hands on you?" Mila jumped in.

"No, no, nothing like that. At least, it didn't get that far—"

"That far!" Mila cried.

"Or it wasn't going to," Lisa quibbled. "I don't know…"

"But what happened?" Veronica prompted.

"It was more an impression than anything particular, y'know? He was angry—with good reason—but then he kinda blew up, and he got up in my face…"

"You get in his face too, sometimes," Veronica observed. "You guys can get into it."

"If that rat bustard touches you…" Mila grumbled.

"What kind of impression, honey?" Veronica asked.

"It was just…I've always felt so safe with Paul, y'know? But the other night, it was the first time…"

"What, you didn't feel safe?" said Mila.

"I don't know *what* I felt. There was a minute there where he got this look in his eyes…"

"Yes?" said Veronica. "What kind of look?"

"I don't know, it's hard to say."

"I think you know," Mila said. "You can tell us, it's all right."

"I don't know, it just reminded me…I guess…I mean, it's silly, I know, but for a second, it was like the kind of look people used to get…in the hood…before they were about to go off somehow. I didn't really think he was going to do anything to me, but I didn't know what he might do neither."

"Wow. Paul?" Veronica mused. "I knew he used to get rough on the streets, but I always thought he was a gentleman to the ladies."

"No such thing as a 'gentleman,'" Mila scoffed. "Oh my, I hate men."

"C'mon, guys, don't be like that," Lisa said. "This is my husband we're talking about. He's a good man. He's just under a lot of stress."

"Will you listen to yourself?" Mila said. "You just got done telling me you don't care what happens to your own mother because of what she did to you, and here V's got a story of some mystery man going after Missy with a bat, and here you go making excuses for your husband when he does the same thing—"

"Paul is *not* the same as my mother!" Lisa snapped.

"Your brother then," Mila returned.

Lisa's eyes grew large and her nostrils flared. She grabbed the table like she needed something to hold onto—or to throw.

"Y'know what? Forget you! You don't know what you're talking about."

The other women were too taken aback to respond right away, and Lisa stood and dug in her purse for her wallet.

"Lisa, don't go," Veronica said weakly. "C'mon!"

"We're done here. I don't need to listen to this stuff from my 'best friends.'" She threw some cash on the table and stormed off.

Mila and Veronica watched her with pained expressions on their faces.

"That did not end well," Veronica said.

"One of these days she's going to do something stupid," Mila said, sadly.

"Yeah, that's what I'm worried about," Veronica said, slowly shaking her head.

They saw Lisa exit the front of the restaurant and try to hail a cab, but the people from the church were taking them all or crowding the road with their cars, so she had to go through the crowd, keeping her eyes focused straight ahead of her as people called after her, saying, "God bless you, sister!"

Lisa took the L back toward her neighborhood where she picked up her car from the lot near the station and drove home. When she arrived, Paul and his friend Rick were in the backyard working on her privacy fence. They were already covered in dirt and sweat and enmeshed in a web of tools and wooden posts.

"Looks to me like you'll be moving the completion date back again," she called from the back door.

Rick and Paul gave her ironic looks and shrugged their shoulders.

"Keeps us out of trouble anyway," Paul said.

"Yeah, I got a whole list of projects to help with that," Lisa responded. "You boys want some lemonade or something?"

"That'd be great, thank you," said Rick. "If you don't have any beer."

"I'll get you all the beer you want when we're done for the day," Paul said. "I need you capable of seeing straight until at least 3:00 p.m."

"Paul, honey, could you come help me, please?" Lisa called, from the kitchen window this time.

Paul and Rick exchanged curious looks. Paul said, "Sure," and Rick winked at him as much to say "Yeah, something's up. Better you than me."

Paul followed Lisa to the kitchen. As he did, he noticed the mail on the table and pointed out a small blue envelope that looked like a card. He decided to open with something lighter.

"That's yesterday's still. You got something from Yolanda. Isn't one of the boys' birthdays coming up?"

"Yeah, maybe. I don't remember."

"They're your nephews…"

"Why's everyone know so much about my family all of a sudden?" Lisa snapped.

"Okay, sorry."

Lisa leaned back against the counter and smiled at him. "No, I'm sorry, baby. I had a little fight with the girls is all. Let's take a drive!"

"A drive? What?"

"Let's just drive! Get out of here a while, enjoy the nice day. You know."

Paul struggled to make sense of what he was hearing. It wasn't only her sudden need to take a drive; it was that on top of feeling like he might at any moment collapse with intolerable pain in his side. He felt like most moments half his mind was occupied with just holding his body together. And now, this?

"What are you talking about? I'm up to my ears in fencing out there."

"Let's go look at houses up on the North Shore like we always talked about."

"Houses?" Paul was genuinely at sea. "Where is this coming from?"

"I got this presentation coming up that should position me to become a director. That'll mean a huge raise, and in another couple years I'll be in line for VP. You're just a year or two from partner…I say we make our move."

She was talking quickly, almost frantically.

"You just told me you wanted a fence, now you want a whole new house?"

"That's what we always dreamed of, right?"

"What would we even do for a down payment? We're in so deep with this house, still."

"We'll figure it out, baby. We got some savings, we got your bonus. Anyway, what's the harm in just looking?"

Paul looked out the window to take a moment to process. Rick was watching some of the neighborhood teenage girls walking down the alley in their booty shorts and crop tops.

"All right," Paul gave in. "We'll go this afternoon."

"No."

"No?"

"It has to be now!"

It seemed to Paul he'd been knocked off his feet and risen only to learn that *up* had become *down*. Either she wasn't usually this irrational or he wasn't usually this distracted.

"I got Rick over..." he said.

"Give him a beer and send him home."

"What's the hurry?"

"Look, all I'm axing is, who's more important to you?"

"All you're *axing*? You're upset. What did they say to you?"

"Would you get off that already?" Lisa was standing up straight now, hands on hips and leaning in as she grew more agitated. "Yeah, we had a little disagreement, *okay*? And then I come home and *ask* my husband to take me for a drive and he puts me off, so maybe I have good reasons for getting a little worked up."

"Fine," Paul said, almost yelling back as they squared off again. "But don't ask me to be rude to my friend. You need to go for a drive so bad, you can go by yourself. I'm going back to build the fence *you 'axed' for*."

Paul marched out of the kitchen and slammed the back door behind him on his way out, leaving Lisa stewing in the middle of the room.

"I take it you didn't get the lemonades," Rick observed as Paul picked up a post.

"I don't know what to do with her sometimes," Paul said. "It's like she suddenly loses her mind."

"Well, y'know..."

"I know what?"

"Just that black women can be pretty demanding," Rick shrugged.

"It's not like that. She's under a lot of stress at work, though. I just don't know how much I'm supposed to put up with at home."

They heard the front door pulled firmly shut, then someone getting into a car and driving off.

"Do you need to be worried about that?" Rick asked with a nod toward the street.

"Nah, she's just blowing off steam."

"As long as she's not blowing somebody else to do it."

Paul dropped the plank he was holding and tried to break Rick's jaw with his fist. Rick fell backward over a stack of planks.

"What the devil, man?" said Rick, pushing himself up to sitting.

"That's *my wife* you're talking about, butthole!" Paul shouted.

For a moment neither said nor did a thing. Their blood was up, and they tried to catch their breaths and figure out what was happening.

"Hey, man," Rick began. "Yeah, you're right. I was way outta line."

"Damn straight you were," Paul confirmed. "C'mon, let's go inside and get those beers."

Rick picked himself up and followed Paul into the kitchen. Paul grabbed two cans of beer from the fridge and held one out to Rick. They sat sipping quietly for a minute.

"Dude, you hit me," Rick said.

"Yeah, I guess I did."

"I never seen you go off on a buddy before is all."

"I've never had a buddy say something like that to me. Buttholes on the force, sure, but not a friend."

"Yo, man…yeah, I'm sorry."

"She's not like that. She's not like those crackheads and street women we used to bust up."

"Okay, man."

"'Okay'? 'Okay,' but what?"

Rick took his time formulating what he wanted to say.

"Let me ask you this: Where do you think she went?" he said.

The question clearly irritated Paul. "She's got this friend who owns a cocktail bar or something over by the ballpark. Her and her girlfriends like to hang out there."

"You like this 'friend,' or is she someone who'd talk stuff about you?"

"*He.* Name's Ennis. I don't know him that well, but I'd guess he's more a sympathetic ear than a fellow gossip."

Rick gave Paul a concerned look. They both knew a sympathetic ear was the worse option.

"Look, I'm only saying this because you're my friend," Rick began again. "We weren't on the force for long, but we saw a lot."

Paul acknowledged that.

"A *lot.* And from what we saw, you know you can take the girl outta the streets, but you can't take the streets outta the girl. That life, growing up like they do, it does something to them."

"*Them* includes my wife and her friends now, Rick," Paul said firmly. "I know these people now. They're *my* friends too. You and I grew up in a pretty rough neighborhood, but we wouldn't put up with any uppity old-money types or whatever telling us we can't live like decent people."

"All right, all right," Rick said, holding his hands out in capitulation. "I won't generalize then. I'll just say that *that woman, your* woman, has something of the street left in her that worries me sometimes."

"Okay," Paul said with authority. "You've had your say. I think it's time we get back to the fence."

"You tha boss."

7

Terrance at Home

Night fell and put the city's troubles to rest for a few hours. The morning broke bright and sunny and hopeful as a fresh peach.

In another part of town, but not so far away as the pigeon flies, Terrance swiveled from the stovetop to the tabletop with a skillet full of scrambled eggs.

"A'ight, boys and girls, ladies and germs, Toms and Jerrys of all shapes and sizes," he announced with a wide toothy grin, "it's time for the moment you've all been waiting for, the main event, full of thrills, spills, and automobills: it's *breakfast*!"

His two sons and baby daughter played their parts and cheered as he dished the eggs onto their plates, singing like Elvis as he did: "That's *one* for my Tommy, *two* for Mike-O, *three* to my baby, now go cats, go!" They dug in with forks and hands; the little girl immediately spilled half of her bowl onto the floor.

"That's all right, baby girl," he said, refilling her bowl. "Rosita will get it." Rosita, a brindled bulldog/boxer mix, was in fact, already licking up the eggs and looking at the highchair in expectation of her next portion.

Terrance continued to sing, "Don't you…step on my blue suede shoes" as he grabbed four slices of toast from the toaster and began to butter them. "Michael, did you finish your homework over the weekend?"

"No, he didn't!" Tommy broke in.

Michael shot back, "You shut up!"

"You were watching TV all afternoon yesterday and you wouldn't stop when Mama told you."

"No, I wasn't!"

"Hold up, hold up," their father said, becoming stern. "You mind your own business, child. I asked your little brother. Now, what's the word, Michael? Is this true?"

Michael had lost some of his enthusiasm for breakfast. "Yes," he admitted.

"A'ight then. You finish up here and then finish up there—or you'll be finished up altogether sooner than later."

"Yes, Daddy."

"Now eat your toast, children. And what do you all want for your lunches?"

"Can we get hot lunch?" Tommy asked.

"*Hot* lunch?" replied his father, still smiling. "*Hot lunch*? I make you this big, lovely, *hot* breakfast, and here you still want a hot lunch?"

"Yeah!" said both boys together. Tommy added, "Mama never lets us."

"Oh boy, oh boy," the man said, shaking his head as if this was the biggest shame he'd ever heard. "You boys know what we used to call 'hot lunch' when I was little? It was when you were so scared a bully was gonna steal your lunch that you broke a sweat wolfing it down fast as could be. Now *that's* a hot lunch."

"Terrance, go on now wit' yourself," said a woman entering from the hallway.

Terrance's smile fell to the floor like the eggs, but with a quick bite of his lower lip he tried to get it back.

"Come 'ere, baby," he said and wrapped an arm around his wife. She avoided a kiss, saying, "Man, I ain't even brushed my teeth yet."

"I don't care, woman. Give me a little something, huh?"

"Da-ad!" Michael moaned.

"You boys watch how to treat your woman right, eh?" he said to them. "It won't make no bit of difference. She gonna spite you. But you got to treat her right nonetheless."

"Where did I find me such a foolish black man?" said Yolanda, kissing him on the cheek as she wormed her way out of his grasp.

"You should be glad you could afford a fool of my caliber," he retorted, smiling his big smile at his kids, who smiled back and shook their heads. Then he took a thin wad of bills from his back pocket and counted some out. He kept one eye on his wife as he did so.

"Here, get your punk selves some hot lunch," he said.

"All right! Thanks, Daddy!" the boys shouted.

"Now you children go get dressed," said their mother.

When the boys had put their plates on the counter and raced away like there was a prize at the top of the stairs, the woman turned to Terrance with folded arms and raised eyebrows.

"T, what are you doing giving those boys money for hot lunch?"

"Aw, come on. What's the harm once in a while?"

"None, if you don't mind going without milk this week."

"I'll get the money."

"Yeah, that's what I'm afraid of." She began to clean up the breakfast dishes.

"C'mon, baby, let's not fight," Terrance said. He came up behind her and put his arms around her stomach. She stiffened at first, hanging on to her irritation, then with a big breath, allowed herself to relax.

"Baby, I don't know how to keep on doing this," she pleaded. "Why can't you get a proper job where I don't have to worry whether you'll come home in your expensive car or a cheap body bag?"

"How you gonna respect a man who wears a noose around his neck and rides the train to a nine-by-five, nine-to-five prison every day? I can guarantee we wouldn't be having any more kids, 'cause even if you could somehow get wet for *me*, I'd hate myself too much to get it up for *you*."

She shrugged out of his embrace again. "Dammit, T, why you gotta talk vulgar like that all the time?"

"It's who I am, baby."

"I don't want those kids hearing you talk that way. Your baby daughter is right there, for goodness sake!"

"She don't know nothing—do you, baby girl?"

"Keep your perverted bedroom-talk for the bedroom, at least."

"Look, I gotta bounce and go earn us some money," he said. "But uh, I gave the boys some of my cash…y'know?"

Yolanda swung around and jutted her hips one way and her shoulders another so her whole body became an incredulous question mark.

"Are you for real? Are you really gonna make me look like the bad guy in front of our children and then have the cojones to ask me for money? You better go take your chances on the street, 'cause you're sure to get yourself killed if you stick around here playing *me* like a dummy."

"A'ight, a'ight, that's how it's gonna be," Terrance said, putting some swagger in his step. "I'll make do, I always have. I just thought a black woman ought to support her man once in a while is all."

"Sometimes she got to support her kids, first, when her man gives them all his money."

Terrance said nothing else, just grabbed the boys' lunches and left the kitchen.

He stood at the foot of the stairs and shouted, "Yo, boys, get your butts in the car! It's time for school!"

The boys came down the stairs in a flurry you could have mistaken for them falling head over heel down each step, but they arrived at the bottom safely, grabbed their lunches from their father's hands, and flew back through the kitchen and out the back door. Terrance walked through the kitchen in silence, but Yolanda stopped him with a mumble and waving something behind her back.

"This is all I got right now, you idiot. You better bring back twice that tonight if you want to keep feeding your kids." She held a small stack of bills out behind her but kept her eyes on the counter. He took them without a word and followed the boys out back.

A garage door opened onto the alley and revealed the stunning kelly-green finish on Terrance's pride and joy: a '74 Dodge Challenger. He could tell you all the specs if you so much as pointed at the thing. He'd bought it well-used, and he had put most of his extra cash into making minor repairs on it for the last six months.

"Michael, get your shoes off my seats!" he said as he got in. The boys were strapped in despite their bouncing around. They liked their dad's car but didn't quite appreciate the status it conferred upon him—or by extension, themselves. They did know enough to become completely silent when their father began backing the wide vehicle out of the narrow garage. Once they hit the road, they could screw around again; that was the rule.

Terrance eased the Challenger back and to the left with great caution, as if he were a far less skillful driver than in fact he was. When they hit the street, the boys both started clamoring for their father's attention, some children's nonsense about video games and the ball game last night and some card game with magical monsters or something. He nodded and asked, "Oh yeah?" and invited them to elaborate as if he understood all that they were going on about, smiling all the while like he'd won the lottery.

If you had told the sixteen-year-old Terrance McNight that by thirty he'd have three kids, be living with their mother, own a sick ride, and be living in a house with a garage (a rental, but nevertheless), he'd have laughed and said, "Man, you're trippin'. I ain't gonna get me stuck with some angry chick inside some white-old picket fence." But what he'd mean was, "No way. A screw-up like me don't get to have that kind of ordinary life."

No, no ordinary life for Terrance McNight, and yet it happened in the ordinary way. He met Yolanda at a party. She was fly in a tight black-and-white striped top and a tighter red skirt. They found a room, did their thing, went their separate ways.

Two days later, he was sitting on his boy Martin's front porch with his crew, and he sees her walking down the street in a navy-blue jump suit, waving at him.

"No way, how'd that chick find me?" he said.

"That that chick from Presto's party?" said Chris C. They called Chris C Chris C to tell him apart from Chris P, whose name became Crispy. This effectively removed the need for differentiation, but Chris C remained Chris C.

"Yeah, she is," Eddie chimed in helpfully. "And she dressed in po-lice blue. You in trouble, boy."

59

His friends thought it about the funniest thing they'd seen in a month of Sundays and began slapping him and groaning and hooting with pleasure.

"Forget you guys! Get me out of here," Terrance said.

"Naw way, man, she seen you already," said Martin.

Terrance shook his head and got up with a sigh then skipped down the stairs and met her with his big smile, saying, "Hey, baby, I didn't know if I'd see you again!"

"That's funny," she said, smiling back with just as much irony. "I left you my number in your pocket."

"Is that right? I musta missed it when I threw my pants in the wash."

"Your jacket pocket," she clarified, standing now toe-to-toe with him. "This jacket, in fact. Here it is." She reached into his pocket and extracted a folded piece of paper.

His crew threw up a cacophony of hoots and howls at what was turning out to be a good show.

Terrance turned to them and shouted, "You fools shut your mouths or I'll kill all y'all!"

"C'mon now, boy, take your medicine!" returned Crispy.

"Don't mind those fools," Terrance told Yolanda.

"What about *this* fool?" she asked and held her finger to his chest like a pistol. They were both smiling for real now.

"Am I under arrest?" he said.

"Are you going to come peacefully?"

"You gonna get rough if I don't?"

"I don't know. You might just like that too much."

"I might just."

"I need to take you down for some questioning."

"That's funny, 'cause I was kinda hoping you might be interested in going down too."

"Your free trial has ended, black man. You want membership to *this* club, you gonna have to pay some dues."

"Damn, girl! You gettin' *me* hard!" yelled Eddie from the porch. The other guys shouted and cheered and punched each other with glee.

"You gonna take me away from these animals, or what?" Yolanda said.

"All right, baby, let's go," he replied, and he didn't even look back at his boys but with a dip of one shoulder sauntered past his new girl and led her to his car. At the time, this was an old black Camaro that was still a couple parts and a paint job away from being as fly as he felt when driving it. He did love that car.

They were a good couple. They had fun together, they liked similar things. Yolanda was good for a couple bucks here and there when he was light.

Then, just a few months in, Yolanda told him she was pregnant. It could have happened that first night. Terrance just about lost it.

"T, I thought you'd be happy!" Yolanda complained.

"What do I need a kid for, woman?"

"What, are you gonna run around the streets all your life? You'll get yourself killed, soon enough, like Andre and Donnie and who knows who else…T, this is our chance to start a family. Start something new and good."

The truth was he wasn't angry so much as excited and scared at the same time. What did he know about raising a child when he hadn't had a dad of his own?

Yolanda understood this on some level, because she gave him an ultimatum: "Terrance, I am not going to raise this child on my own. He needs a daddy. So until you put a ring on this finger, you can consider this girl and this purse is closed for business."

Terrance hustled and pulled together the money for a ring. They moved in together, and then a couple months after that they were in the hospital holding a little cocoa-colored boy wrapped tight in a blanket. The marriage thing kept getting pushed back until things settled down a bit, but things never settled down.

"He's so little," Terrance whispered when they first met their son, Tommy. He tried to worm his finger into the infant's closed fist.

"This is good, right?" Yolanda asked. "We made this. We did something good."

"Yeah, baby. That's right," he said.

"Have a good day at school now! Learn your reading and writing," Terrance told his boys as he pulled up to the curb outside their school. The boys yelled "Bye, Daddy!" and hopped out the passenger side while Terrance held the front seat down for them. He watched them until each of them joined a group of friends as if they'd always been there. It was good for kids to have friends, but he liked that they still liked driving with him. After a moment's appreciation, he drove off.

He headed two blocks west then turned south through a neighborhood that would connect to an artery street that would take him to the corner he liked to work. All of a sudden, he heard two dull percussions, at which he slammed his brakes and ducked behind the dashboard. He heard glass break, smelled smoke. Then he heard someone shouting his name. Someone he recognized.

He put the car in park right in the middle of the street and burst out the door. He saw his assailant on the sidewalk fifty feet away, his gun pointed down and looking more for a fight than to shoot it again. That was good, because Terrance was in a fighting mood.

"Domino? Crazy fool, what the hell you doin'?" he shouted, marching toward the man.

"You owe my man money, T!"

"There's a school just over there, man!" Terrance said. "You gonna kill some kid."

Domino obviously had not thought about that.

"Ain't no kids here," he said. "Just a crackhead who still owes us two stacks."

"Well, you gonna kill *me* then! Try to get your money from a dead man, you dummy!"

Domino obviously had not thought about this, either. Domino was not the type to have thought about much. By this time Terrance had approached within ten feet of the man, from which distance they stood eying each other warily while trying to act like they weren't. The curtains in windows up and down the block were pulled back momentarily then released. This wasn't the kind of neighborhood that dialed 911, but they wanted to know what was going on.

"Yeah, well, I'm sorry 'bout that." Domino said after watching another curtain fall into place. "But that's water under the bridge, man. You owe Big George for that car."

"That car? You mean my car over there? You mean that car you just shot up? You *shot. My. Car!*"

"Far as Big George is concerned it's still *his* car."

"And how's he gonna feel about you shooting up his car?"

Now Domino was really confused. He opted to go back on the attack.

"Where's the blanking money, man?"

"Man, you know I'mma get his money."

"S'not fast enough, man. Big George keeps hearing about you tricking out your ride rather than paying him what's his. He don't like looking like a soft touch."

"I got a deal going down *today*, man…high-class stuff. We got a new in with some stupid rich white kids who will *pay* for this stuff. I'm telling you…"

Terrance did his best to keep the pleading out of his voice, but he clearly didn't want to be on Big George's bad side.

"Big George don't like waiting. What you got on you now?"

"What I got is what I need to buy more inventory, man. Don't you understand business?"

"I understand paying your debts. I understand making a fool of someone who takes a chance on you. I understand getting dropped. Now what you got, man?"

"Aw, man," Terrance whined as he reached for his back pocket. The man tightened his grip on the gun. "Chill, man. It's just my clip," Terrance scoffed, producing the money clip held between two fingers. He pulled out all the bills, quickly glanced at how much he was handing over and huffed and moaned to make it clear this was a great injustice.

"It's not much," the man said.

"Well, I was planning to turn it into more."

"We could repossess the car…"

"Just…just give me some more time. I'll pay, man. You know I'll pay."

"You got a good rep for paying your debts, T," the man nodded with a smile.

"Fat lot of good it does me when some dumb boy's gonna come shoot up my car anyway," Terrance complained.

"This will buy Big George's good will, T. That and those bullet holes. Don't worry about it. I'll vouch for you."

"Yeah, thanks a ton, Domino. Just make sure that all gets to Big George. I don't want to fund your next blow job."

Domino put his pistol into his coat pocket now that it had cooled off enough then walked away. Terrance shuffled back to his poor car, demoralized. There was a bullet hole in the hood and the passenger window had a hole in the middle of a crystalline spider web. He searched the cab for the bullet and found it sunk into the back seat.

Right where Tommy had been sitting.

Terrance fell into the seat and sat there in shock. In his mind he fought to keep his focus on the task ahead, scrounging up the money he needed to make his deal that afternoon. But the image of that bullet hole in the back seat kept crowding in until he could feel tears, the release of coiled fear, pushing against his eyes and throat. His breathing grew deeper and more deliberate, he closed his eyes. He had half a mind to let it hit him. Something like a tear formed in his left eye.

From behind him came the irate honking of a motorist who'd just turned onto the street. Some guy who didn't care what happened, he just wanted to get where he was going. He laid on the horn and yelled out his window. Terrance came to his senses, held his middle finger out his window then drove away to get down to the business of the day.

8

Hot on the Streets

9:56 a.m.

Terrance stood before a derelict warehouse. Some kind of old shoe factory or something. He'd parked his Charger a couple blocks away through a couple alleys. He looked impatient, kept checking his watch, looking up and down the street. Every time a car passed he'd sort of stretch his back a bit and hop a little like he'd just gotten there, but the cars kept passing him up.

The sun shone bright, warming the late morning air.

10:37 a.m.

"Oh man, where he at?" Terrance muttered to himself. He kicked the sidewalk, kicked the streetlamp, kicked the corrugated steel side of the building. He paced up and down the whole block just to pass the time. He shrugged off his jacket and threw it over a fire hydrant.

Several crows perched on the power line in the alley beside the building and eyed the pigeons in the dumpster.

10:44 a.m.

A car approached. Terrance slowed his steps and sauntered back to his spot. The car pulled up, but it wasn't who Terrance was expecting.

"Hey, if it ain't the Marlboro Man!" Terrance said with a toothy grin. "What up, dog?" The Marlboro Man didn't seem quite so happy to see Terrance.

"Hey, Teeball," he grunted, using one of the nicknames he knew Terrance hated. "Big George waitin' on his stacks."

"What, you think I don't know that? What you think I'm doing here on the street in the damn sun? This a big deal going down, you'll see. I'mma get his money."

"Well, you don't gotta tell me, man," Marlboro grumbled, tossing his head back indifferently. "I'm just relaying a message."

"Yeah, well, Domino already give me enough messages for a while."

"Domino a screw up."

"Man, you said it, not me," Terrance said, laughing.

"Don't you be laughing at Domino, dog."

"Aw, man, c'mon. You know I don't mean nothing by it."

"Don't tell me what I know," Marlboro said and drove off.

"A'ight, a'ight," T said as if he could be heard. "You want to play it that way, that's a'ight. I thought we was all friends here, but I guess it's the times or something…"

11:17 a.m.

It was beginning to get hot now. Terrance was sweating through his T-shirt. A car approached. He tried to act cool. The car passed. It looked like he could start crying.

12:36 p.m.

Terrance slid through the door of Queen Phoebe's Beauty and Supply like it said "Property of King Terrance" out front. But then, he entered every place like that.

"Ladies, ladies, ladies, you are looking *fly* today!" he proclaimed, holding his arms wide in blessing.

"Hey, baby," Yolanda said without looking up from her customer's head.

Terrance bobbed over to his woman and tried to kiss her, but she avoided him with just her head while freezing her hands where they were.

"Not now, T!"

"I'm just trying to show my girl some love, baby," he said. He held himself at an angle, slightly dipping from the knees and waist, showing his audience how preternaturally comfortable he was in the world.

"And I'm trying not to burn Mrs. Prince's scalp!" his wife shot back.

"Ha! *Misses Prince's.* Misses Prince's Pepper-mintses! Fresh as the day the doctor spanked her cute little baby behind!"

"Go on!" said the ladies, and "Fresh!" and "I'mma tell your mama you talking like that 'round here!"

They rolled their eyes and *tsk-tsk*ed like they had no patience for this man-boy, but their smiles egged him on.

"How's it going, Veronica?" he called. "Pretty as a plum and just as sweet! (Or so I imagine.)" He winked for everyone to see, and Veronica blushed even darker like she did every time he said that.

Veronica's chair was conveniently located at the far end of the salon from Yolanda's, and he made his way down between the rows complimenting each woman's braids or waves or colors until he was right beside her admiring her work on Asia Jackson's hair.

"Tell him *no*, V," Yolanda shouted from her chair by the window.

Terrance scowled and waved her off.

"It's so hard to find a black woman who will support her man," he said confidentially.

"Maybe because it's so hard to find a black man who ain't always asking his woman for money," Veronica suggested.

"Ouch!" said Terrance and mimicked being shot in the heart. "But a'ight, a'ight, I know there's truth in that statement, though it hurts to admit it. Brothers be sponging off they women coz they don't have any business acumen, you feel me?"

"T, I ain't never felt you, and you ain't never gonna feel this," said Veronica, gesturing to her large curves. She gave Asia a slow-sliding five.

"Y'all can turn the A/C off coz you's cold enough without it. Anyway, I'm trying to say I ain't here for money. I'm here for *capital*."

Even Asia couldn't stop herself from joining the chorus of women exclaiming, *Ha!* at that one.

"Hear me out, hear me out. I got a lead on some merchandise a guy down state wants to move, but he can't leave town on account of his parole. So he's willing to let it go cheap to anyone who will come and get it. I got the wheels. I just need a couple hundred more dollas so I can buy it off him. Once I flip it, you'll get your investment back *with interest*."

"Yeah, well, I'm gonna need it because I have no interest in this conversation right now," Veronica said.

"That's right, V," Yolanda murmured with a comb in her mouth.

"Yo, woman, would you just lay off, already?" T shouted back. "Look, V, this is quality product, the kind of stuff I can sell downtown or, maybe, in the burbs, at a premium. We all gonna make a lot of money off of this."

V put her comb down and drew close to Terrance so she could speak quietly.

"Listen, T, I don't think you want to do this here. You already in the hole with me for almost a hundred dollars I don't expect to ever see again, and I *know* you don't want me making no fuss about it."

Terrance winced, but he wasn't defeated.

"You right, you right," he whispered back. "That's on me, okay? That's on me. But this deal, it's real, and I'mma be in big trouble with some rough characters if I don't do something *tout de suite*. Puh-*lease*, V."

He could see her softening, but she said, "T, even if I wanted to—which I don't because Yolanda said not to—I don't have it. I'm dry."

"Don't have what? A couple Benjamins? It's okay, one is fine. Even half a yard'll do. I'll make up the rest."

At this point, all the women in the shop were staring at him, and he didn't like what they were seeing.

"No, T," Veronica said as gently as possible. She returned to Asia's hair and apologized to her for the distraction. T tried to maintain some level of dignity and saunter out smiling and pointing at the ladies as he did, but the playful spirit with which he'd entered had been drowned in Barbicide at the back of the shop and everyone knew it.

"How *do* you do it, 'Landa?" the women said, but Yolanda just kept working, working.

9

Terrance Comes Over

A Monday had rarely been more welcome to Lisa. She'd spent much of Sunday drinking Irish coffees at Ennis's bar before cooling down enough to go back home. She apologized to Paul, but she sensed something was still bothering him; she just didn't want to deal with drama from him, of all people.

Jazmin Darwish practically moved into Lisa's office for the week. They spent every minute when they weren't in a meeting going over reports and graphs and creating lists of taglines and concepts. They drank gallons of coffee and ordered their lunches in. They had to replace notepads and pens and take power naps in the afternoon. Their colleagues would walk by and see them through the floor-to-ceiling windows and try to hide little double takes. They'd been waiting for these two to become friends, had always been confused why they hadn't become close immediately, and now that they were together the world made sense again.

Lisa noticed this more than Jazmin, who usually sat on a small sofa with her back to the windows. She held it against her at first, but while Jazmin was a little green and maybe overzealous, she worked hard, asked good questions, and Lisa genuinely liked her. Their mutual marginality created a kind of safe haven within the office. They could joke about how buttoned up these white people were, share horror stories about the casual racism they'd experienced, and even compare notes on finding the right shades of lipstick.

Paul, meanwhile, got wrapped up in his big new client. For the first half of the week, she didn't see him until he got into bed beside her, or vice versa. They'd talk on the phone during their lunch or dinner hours, but otherwise it was hard to feel very connected. She had to remind herself that they'd had seasons like this in the past and they'd always come through them; they didn't last forever.

These seasons were, if anything, the cost of the lives they chose. Careers over family. Upward mobility. Respectable middle-class status.

Or so she told herself. During the day, she'd be consumed with the problems of the day. It seemed like that was all that was important. But when Paul fell back onto the bed late at night and she put her hand on his arm or hip, electricity flowed through her body and she realized how much she missed him, how much she needed even simple touches.

She didn't say anything about Terrance asking for money or the news that her mother had been sick. She didn't say anything about Yolanda or her nephews and niece possibly being in any danger. Nor did Paul say anything about his diagnosis. This was how they convinced themselves that the testiness each had with the other, so rare over the nine years they'd been together, was really about stress at work.

On Wednesday night, they crashed into one another, wordless and hungry. They consumed one another and then fell apart, and each felt nagged by the thought that it could have been anyone. To compensate, they began to plan their next vacation, and they laughed when, on Thursday night, they each came home next night with a little gift for the other.

Lisa had bought a six-pack of Paul's favorite beer when she stopped at the store for a few odd things. A small-enough votive offering for a devoted wife to make.

Paul thanked her, but when she offered to bring him one right away, he declined.

"You all right, baby?" she asked.

"Yeah, my stomach just hurts a bit."

"Okay…You need some Tylenol?"

"Already took some. It usually goes away after a little while."

"What do you mean 'usually'? You've had this before? Baby, that sounds like something you should get checked out."

Paul grunted and waved her off.

She frowned and went to the kitchen. The bottles chimed together much too cheerfully for her mood as she put the beer in the fridge.

"I don't suppose you're going to be up for anything later then, huh?" she called half-heartedly.

"Huh? Oh, I don't know. I hope so."

But it was already late and they both fell asleep watching TV on the couch.

Friday was the day Daisy would come and clean their house. Daisy was a lady from a few blocks over who cleaned several of the houses in their neighborhood. She was Lisa's idea. Lisa hated doing housework; it reminded her too much of what she thought of as her Cinderella upbringing. Her mother conscripted her to do all manner of chores around the house, never minding if she had homework or wanted to see a friend. This was her mama's way of preparing her for being a woman in this world, but now that Lisa had some money, she didn't have to accept that way of seeing things.

Paul, meanwhile, felt uncomfortable paying a black woman to clean his house, so he often left by six or six thirty in the morning to avoid seeing Daisy arrive at seven. Lisa worked so late most nights that she often went in late on Friday mornings, and despite the pile of work she had on her desk, she decided to take her time and enjoy her coffee and appreciate her garden, which was producing copious tomatoes and beans and looked promising for carrots and squash.

The truth was, she wasn't thinking about her beans and carrots or the squirrels that tried to eat them but about the fight she and Paul had had the previous week. The fight when he broke the plate. She wasn't used to Paul objecting to anything. Nothing got to him.

Until now. Which meant something had changed; something was wrong. And since the primary thing that she could identify had changed was her increasing absorption at work and neglect of him, she had to blame herself. What was the point of all the money she was making if she couldn't keep her man happy?

Daisy always found a way to clean in some room Lisa didn't need at the moment and would be done quick if for some reason Lisa entered. Now she was in front somewhere doing the windows.

What must her life be like, Lisa thought, *taking care of other people's homes?* Was her own home clean, or did she not have time for that? Was it nice to set your own hours and at the end of the day be done with it, or was it always a slog? Did she think Paul and Lisa were slobs, or entitled, or what? Paul hadn't wanted to hire her, but Lisa figured they paid her a fair wage, so what was the problem?

Just one more way she and Paul didn't see eye to eye. Why did it seem so difficult sometimes? Was this the kind of thing that drove couples to therapy?

Before she knew it, the cordless was in her hands and she was dialing Mila. Mila never went in to work before eleven o'clock. Mila would know what to do.

Mila picked up after the fifth ring.

"Hi, honey, did I wake you up?" Lisa said.

"It's not even 8:00 a.m.," Mila said. "Of course you woke me up. What's up?"

"We can talk later if you'd like…"

"No, no, it's fine."

"You ever been to therapy? Like with a psychiatrist or whatever?"

"No, but I know lots of folks who have. My parents did. My brother's been in therapy since he was, like, sixteen. What do you want to go to therapy for?"

"I don't know that I do. It just feels silly to me, though, sitting there talking about your problems with some stranger…I don't know."

"Lisa, if it means saving your marriage, it's probably worth feeling silly."

"Who said anything about 'saving' my marriage? We're just under some stress is all."

"Uh-huh."

"Now what do you mean by that?"

73

"Nothing, never mind," Mila said. "Look, if you're asking, it probably means you should go."

"I don't know if I'm ready."

"Well, you wanted my advice. I gave it."

"Yeah—what in the world?"

Lisa heard someone banging on her front door like they were trying to bust through it.

"I better go. Lunch, Saturday at one? Okay, honey, see you then."

Daisy opened the front door to Terrance, wearing a tank top and a do-rag.

"Yes?" she said.

"Who the hell are you?" the man said.

"I'm Daisy. I clean Ms. Lisa's house Fridays. Is there something I can do for you?"

Terrance scoffed and chuckled to himself, rocking back in disbelief.

"You clean Lisa *house*? That's too funny. Don't you know we free? I'm her brother, Terrance," he said and began to let himself in. "I gotta talk to my sister."

Daisy tried to block him but he was too strong for her.

"Mr. Terrance, let me tell her you're here!"

"Nah, that's a'ight, I'll find her. And hey, I'll put in a good word for *you*, too. We gone get you some papers."

At this point, Lisa had come into the dining room and seen him.

"What do you want, Terrance? Why are you banging on my door?"

"Man, how come you always locking your door? This is a nice, safe neighborhood, isn't it?" Terrance answered. "And why you put a nice black woman to work for you?"

"I pay her good money," she said then added, "Not that it's any of your business."

Terrance sauntered into the kitchen and started rooting in the pantry.

"I'm sorry, Ms. Lisa," Daisy said. "He pushed his way in."

"It's fine, Daisy. Why don't you just go home early."

"You sure?"

"Yeah, you don't want to be here for this."

As Daisy was packing her things, Lisa walked into kitchen yelling, "Now, T, don't you have food in your own house?"

"Not like the food you got in your house." Terrance pulled out a bag of cookies. "Damn, now these are some fancy cookies!"

Lisa wanted to be angry with him, but she had a hard time staying angry when he got that big wide grin on his face. It was so childish, genuine. So unlike most of the things he said and did.

"It's Michael's birthday coming up," he said and popped a cookie in his mouth. "You coming to the party?"

"Yeah, maybe, I don't know," Lisa said, but as she did, she was looking at the door jamb from the hall to the kitchen and suddenly concerned about something she found there.

"You always too busy to come to your own nephews' parties," Terrance said simply. "And baby Tammy's gonna be one in a few months too, you know."

"Yeah, I know."

"We named her after you. Your middle name."

"I know. It's a real honor and all. Paul and I are just busy a lot of the time, you know?"

Talking to Terrance could go like this. You'd begin expecting a fight, but then he'd get you feeling bad about yourself without even trying to, and then...

"Hey, Lise, look..." he began.

And then it would turn into the fight you were expecting.

"I know, I know," said Lisa. "The money."

At this point, she was walking away to the front hall just to have something to do that wasn't wringing his neck.

"Lise, sis—" he started to call after her.

"Oh, no, don't start with that 'sis' business. I don't wanna hear none of *that*," she shouted back.

"C'mon, this is *serious*," he said, following her into the front of the house. He left the cookies in the kitchen, at least.

"It's *always* serious, T," Lisa sighed. "I can't handle how serious you always are when you come round needing my money."

"I just gotta do this one deal, and then I'll be set for a few weeks. I got some things lined up. I'm trying here, but, Yolanda…"

Lisa sat down on the stairs to the second floor and put her head in her hands.

"I can imagine what Yolanda's feeling, believe me. But Terrance—when is it gonna end?"

It wasn't the first time she'd asked the question, but it never failed to make him pause, to break, if only briefly, through the indomitable energy that typified his being in the world. He leaned against the front door and looked everywhere except in her eyes.

"Maybe tonight, y'know? I don't know. If I can just get Big George off my back…"

"*Big George?*" Lisa said. "Last time it was Tiny Tony or something, wasn't it? And then there was Lupe Six and before that Alessandro Something-or-other. I can't keep up with all the trouble you get into."

A sort of hang-dog look came over Terrance as she spoke. You could see the life force struggling to strain on even as her words kept tearing away at it. He didn't know any way to deal with it other than to press forward, always forward.

And that's what could make him dangerous.

"Yeah, well, look, sis," he said, shaking the swagger back into his shoulders. "I know you think I'm a dumb-butt, and maybe I am, okay? But we're blood, y'know? We're brother and sister, a'right? And that *means something*. At least, it does to *me*. If it don't mean nothing to you, then you better say it, and I guess I'll have to be on my way. But if bein' blood still stands for something, then maybe you can quit with the sermons and we can talk real business for a minute."

But Lisa didn't want to talk at all. She had enough on her mind to be dealing with Terrance's nonsense too.

"T, I want you out of my house."

"What you say?"

"I said, I want you out. Of. My. House."

Terrance shifted from foot to foot and shook his head like he couldn't believe his ears.

"Now, I know you ain't gonna do me like that in my time of need. You the one told me to come by now. I'm your brother, after all," he said, and he flashed her his big toothy grin, but it was the phony, manipulative version that she had been wise to since days long gone by. Strangely, she saw behind it something like fear, the jittery, edgy quality Yolanda had told her friends about. She didn't quite know what it meant, but her gut told her it wasn't good. She just wanted him gone.

"Do you know what's gonna happen to me and my family if I don't get some cash together?" he said, suddenly sober.

Lisa took a deep breath and, after a moment's hesitation, determined to stick to her guns.

"I said all I got to say, T. Go. Please," she said. She rose and walked upstairs.

"Hey!" Terrance shouted. "Lisa! Now wait a minute! Ain't nobody gonna turn their back on *me*!"

"I ain't your nobody, T," she said without turning to him.

Next thing she knew, he was behind her and grabbing her arm. He tried to swing her around, but she resisted and wrenched free then jogged the last couple steps to the next floor.

"Terrance, you better get your butt out of my house!" she warned. But he wasn't in the mood for warnings. He followed her upstairs and into her bedroom. "T, I'm warning you..."

"You're 'warning me'?" he said, visibly and genuinely hurt. "You're '*warning* me'? Lise, I thought we was blood relations. I thought we looked out for each other."

"Yeah, well, maybe I'm tired of doing all the looking out without getting much looking out for," she snapped back, and as soon as the words left her mouth he had swung his open palm and slapped her across the face. It made a shocking *smack* sound that made them exchange looks of surprise.

"Who..." Terrance began, trying to stay in control of the situation, "who do you think you are? I don't look out for you? Where did all...*this* come from?" He indicated the house and all her things. "Who made all this *possible*? I don't look out for you? Forget you!"

"Forget you!" Lisa shot back. "I worked for what I have, and I don't need some deadbeat punk dopehead mooching off me because he sold a few grams of weed back in the day!"

It was too much for him. He flew at his sister, intent on doing some kind of harm—just what and how much he could not have said.

She felt several slaps and punches as she dodged him and ran about the room. She made her way to Paul's side of the bed. A blow to the back sent her to her knees, but now she was at Paul's bedside table. She quickly pulled the drawer open, reached in, and pulled out his old service revolver. Before she could think, she was pointing it at her brother and rising to her feet.

"Aw, no, no," Terrance was saying, trying to act cool, trying to laugh. "I know you're not pointing no piece at me, at your brother!"

"I don't know what else to call this, T," she said.

"For real, girl, put it down. This is whack."

"No," she said. "No, I don't think so."

They stood staring at each other and the gun, both of them surprised by what was happening. Both poised for some action, who knew what. Then Terrance's whole demeanor shifted, and he became like a whipped puppy.

"What you gonna do? You gonna shoot me? You gonna shoot your brother? Your own flesh and blood?"

"No," Lisa spat. "Don't pull that 'flesh and blood' crap on me. You come in my house, asking me for money, beating me up?" She was starting to cry.

"Look, I'm sorry, okay? I got a little rough, there. A'ight? I'm under a lot of pressure out there. But it's cool. We cool. Now come on put that down and let's talk like adults."

"I...I don't think so," Lisa said. She hardly knew what she was saying. She hardly knew what she was doing. But she could still feel his fist hitting her back, hitting a wound so deep she had forgotten it was there. And his every slimy word wove a net around her she had thought she'd long escaped.

"T...I want...I want you to leave my house," Lisa stammered. "I want you to leave my house, and I don't want to see your sorry butt here again without an invitation. You got that?"

"What are you saying? Are you even listening to yourself?" Terrance seemed legitimately confused.

"*Now.*"

He started side-stepping out of the room and backing toward the stairs.

"Yeah, okay. All right. Have it your way. I mean…I mean, *Lise!* It's me! It's T, your brother!"

"Keep moving," she said, following him from a distance of ten paces with the pistol pointed at his chest.

"This is a mistake," he said, affecting confidence and authority. "You're going to regret this."

"I'll regret it more if I give you one more freaking dollar to blow on those stupid drugs of yours," she replied.

Terrance had backed himself to the front door. Lisa stopped at the foot of the stairs. He reached behind him and opened it and started to exit.

"Lise, listen to me," he said, and something in his voice made her listen. Something in his tone told her she had pushed him across a line, and if she really ran him out of her house at the end of her husband's gun it was not going to go well for her.

"Lise, listen to me. If you do this, if you run me off at gunpoint, there's no going back. I won't forget something like this. I can't. It's life or death for me out there. I came here a supplicant, asking you for a few bucks to help me keep me and my family safe, and you're telling me that you're just as dangerous as those fools out there who have it in for me."

"Just go," she said, but it was in a hoarse whisper. Tears rolled down her face.

"Sis, it ain't gonna end well for you. You'll be sorry for this. I'll see to that."

"Go."

He was crying too now. He didn't want things to go this way. She could see it but she couldn't stop it. She knew as well as he did that he had to do what he had to do.

"Lise…Sis…" True sadness flooded his face, but it fought with a deeply ingrained code, the code of the streets. He couldn't make her see. "Lise, I'm sorry. I'm sorry it has to be this way. You're dead to me. You're dead."

"T, you better go," was all she could say.

"You're dead. You're dead."

He let the door swing open as he left. He walked slowly across the lawn to his kelly green Challenger, repeating "You're dead" softly to himself as he did.

Lisa tried to keep herself from calling him back. The look on his face frightened her like nothing ever had before. *Maybe,* she thought, *he was really in too deep, this time. Maybe he would snap somehow.*

The last thing she thought as he drove away was that it looked like a bullet hole in that perfect green hood.

10

Protection

Lisa was useless the whole rest of the day. She was late, which was unlike her, and everyone picked up on the fact that her head wasn't in it that day.

She'd never seen her brother quite so upset. She knew he was capable of surprising violence, and she'd seen him go off even on friends. She flashed back to the time his friends had come over and were just hanging out in front of the house playing music on a car stereo. Terrance was in a bad mood that day and wasn't even outside with them.

Mama yelled from the porch for them to go on somewhere else, that Terrance wasn't coming out, but they didn't go nowhere. Then Terrance came out on the porch and told them he wasn't coming out that day and didn't his mama say for them to bounce? His friends acted all disappointed but were laughing and joking around and didn't budge an inch. Maybe five minutes later Terrance came storming out of the house with a baseball bat, went right up to Anton Jackson, and smashed his jaw with the bat, yelling, "My mama told you to get out of here!"

The Jacksons were old family friends. They didn't press charges or anything, only asked that the McNights pay for the medical bills.

She'd heard tell of her brother beating up guys who'd wandered into the wrong territory, of random violence to property just to blow off steam.

Then there was the firefight in a Jewel-Osco parking lot. Two guys got shot. One died, the other spent a couple months in prison. Lisa had heard Terrance was involved, may have even started it—or that, at least, he had put down the first victim. But no one else was arrested or charged. They never even announced a suspect.

In over a decade of living the life, Terrance had never spent more than an evening in lockup. No one had ever tried to hold him accountable to his actions, and now she had wronged him.

And how. Where had that come from? She'd thought she had put that kind of thing behind her when she left home. In fact, she'd worked to extract and expunge the parts of herself that knew how to fight back like that. She hardly ever raised her voice and never dreamed of threatening harm to anyone. But when Terrance started roughing her, it all came back like it had never really left.

No, not just Terrance. The hood in her had reared its ugly head lately with Paul. Whatever was going on with him triggered a primal reaction in her. She fought it down the best she could, but if they didn't work things out, he might see a side of her he would not like at all.

Meanwhile, Jazmin tried to hide her irritation, but she had to constantly repeat herself and carried most of the day's work on her own. By mid-afternoon she'd had enough, and she let Lisa know it. Lisa had no excuse and didn't have any fight in her, but she knew she needed to be decisive.

"Look, Jazmin, you're right. I'm no good right now. I need to attend to some things to get my head back on straight." She created a task list and asked Jazmin if she could handle a set of them on her own for a day or so then left for the day.

There wasn't actually much she could do with what was left of the afternoon. She stopped at Ennis's place and asked him to make her something to cheer her up.

"Try this," he said and handed her a limoncello sour.

"It's good," she told him. "How do you do it?"

"Experience, intuition, and a little luck," he said with a coy smile. "But I ain't gonna lie: most people are just happy to have a little alcohol in front of them."

They chuckled together at this. It was true; she just wanted someone to take care of her and give her a drink.

"Ennis, you ever get in any trouble with anyone?" she asked him. "Like, on the streets?"

"Sure. Why, what happened?"

She gave him the brief version.

"What, girl, that's bad," he sighed. "But this your brother we talking about."

"That's the thing, it didn't look like him. His eyes…they were crazy, all big and red and wild…"

"Was he high already?"

"Maybe coming down, but he wasn't acting high, just crazy."

"Do you want me to try to talk to him?"

"No, thank you. I shouldn't have even told you. If he finds out anyone else knows, he'll freak even worse."

Ennis reached across the bar and put his hand on hers.

"It's gonna be okay. Give him a day or so then call him and apologize. Maybe give him a few bucks—that's probably the quickest way."

"If only…"

Paul was furious when she told him. She almost didn't say anything; she preferred to handle her family on her own. The less Paul saw of them, the better, she figured. More information about them would do nothing to improve the picture he got of them from back when he was working that neighborhood.

Even more than that, however, was the fact that she was surprised and embarrassed at herself for going for Paul's gun. He had shown her how to use it for protection, but neither of them really expected her to use it at all, much less on her own brother. Was she really capable of doing what she had threatened? Was she not who she thought she was?

So she told him what she thought was most important to know.

"Terrance came by today, Paul," she said as she was going through the mail.

"Yeah? What did he want?" Paul was reading some file or other, though it looked like he was having difficulty concentrating.

"What's he ever want?" she scoffed.

"How much did you give him?"

"Nothing," Lisa said and opened another envelope.

"Really? I don't expect he liked that."

"No, he did not." She gave herself a couple breaths to prepare for the next bit. "In fact, he got a little rough with me."

"What?" Paul put down his file.

"It's fine. It's over," she said, though her voice betrayed the growing realization of just what had happened to her. "I dealt with him. Kicked him out."

"Wait, what do you mean, 'got rough'? Did he touch you?"

Lisa dropped the mail and began to cry. A real, defenses-down kind of cry. Paul leapt up and came to comfort her.

"That bastard!" he muttered. "I'll...I don't know what."

Lisa gathered herself and shook her head.

"Don't do nothing. I just need you with me."

"Look at you! You're afraid," Paul objected. "I can't let him do this to you and just look the other way. I...I'm going over there!"

He jumped up and was heading for the door when Lisa called him back.

"Don't you dare!" she shouted, suddenly afraid. "I don't want you playing Superman and getting yourself hurt."

"You don't think I can handle your brother?"

"No! It's just, you need to be careful."

"Dammit!" Paul pounded the air.

"Look, let me handle Terrance. I got it."

"What are you going to do: fight him?"

"I'll get a restraining order."

Lisa hadn't admitted to herself that she was even considering this until she said it out loud, and she said it with hesitation and embarrassment. It just wasn't what people did where she came from—but she wasn't from there anymore.

"A *restraining order*?" Paul couldn't quite believe what he was hearing. "I don't even know where to start with that. But that won't matter to a guy like Terrance, baby."

"Well, I'm not going to let you fight him, and I'm not going to pay him off like Ennis said."

"You've already talked to Ennis about this?"

"You were at work."

"I'm your *husband!*"

"Paul, please don't start this…"

But it had started. The old familiar fight. He said she didn't trust him; she said she was devoted to him. He said he felt like a visitor in her life; she said she left everything to make a life with him, and so on. Lisa wasn't unsympathetic to his feelings, but she had made a promise to herself years ago never to back down from a fight when she was in the right.

"I don't want you going round Ennis's place again," he said after ten or fifteen minutes of this.

"Excuse me?"

"You heard me."

"Well, I hope I heard wrong, 'cause it sounded like you were giving me an order."

"I'm your husband. I have some rights, I think."

"You have the right to shut your mouth about now, I'd say." They were both standing now, and she was feeling glorious in her indignation. Maybe the hood was still down in there, but it was the part of her that had its limits of how many people in her life could try to keep her down. "I'm not about to sit here and let some white boy get uppity with *me*," she snapped—and immediately regretted it.

"Ah! So it's like that! I suppose I have ways of making you respect me, if that's what you're going to need."

"Paul, honey, that came out wrong," she whimpered, but it was too late. Without a word, he turned and stalked out of the room and out of the house. Two hours later she heard a car pull up to the front of the house. She pulled the curtain back a tad to watch as Ennis pulled her husband out of the passenger side of his car and half carried him to the front door. But something was wrong. Ennis was beating on the front door and calling for her.

She raced downstairs and let him in.

"He just started grabbing his stomach and moaning," Ennis said as he pulled Paul in. Paul was clutching his side and wincing. "He wouldn't let me call an ambulance."

"*Oh my god, oh my god,*" Lisa cried as she helped Ennis lay Paul down on a couch. "What's wrong, baby? Maybe I should take him anyway? What do I do?"

"No…hospitals…" Paul spat. "Bedside…table…"

Lisa ran up to his bedside table and pulled open the drawer to find boxes and vials of medications that she had not known were there. For a moment she could do nothing but stare. She began to turn them over and read the labels. Peach ellipses marked BUMEX, a box labeled CINACALCET HYDROCHLORIDE, a vial of little white oval pills stamped VICODIN.

Her instinct for saving her husband kicked back in, and she took the Vicodin back down to Paul. Ennis helped her get one down his throat with a couple sips of water.

"You might as well get back to your bar," Lisa told her friend. "There's nothing left for me to do but wait."

"You have any idea what's going on?"

"He was complaining of pain in his side a while ago. I told him to see a doctor, but he never told me anything else."

"All right, well, I'll call you later."

He dashed out the door and she was alone with her ailing husband. She made some tea for them both. By the time it was ready his color was returning and his breathing slowed down. He even sat up a bit on the couch. She sat with him until he had returned to normal and made him promise to see a doctor, which after a moment's hesitation, he did. But the sad look on his face worried her. She knew he hated to appear weak in front of her, that he wanted to be strong physically as well as emotionally. How could she convince him that she could be strong for him, too?

11

TV Time

It was dark when Terrance drove up to his house. He parked in front rather than in the garage, and he emerged with a set look to his face.

He marched in to find things as he had anticipated them. Yolanda was in the kitchen cleaning up after dinner and the boys were watching TV in the living room.

"Where you been, baby?" Yolanda called. "You didn't tell me you was gonna miss dinner."

Terrance didn't answer but walked into the living room.

"Sorry, kids, but I need this TV," he announced and turned the unit off. The boys shouted in protest, but their father ignored them and hoisted the set into his arms.

"T, what the hell you doin'?" Yolanda said, entering the room.

"Nothing. I'll bring it back in a bit," Terrance said.

"The boys was watching that! What are you doing?"

"I said I'll bring it back!"

Terrance began to walk out, but Yolanda stood in his way. The boys took their mother's resistance as a cue and began to slap at their father and pull at his shirt. Terrance wasn't in a position to defend himself, but he managed to kick out at them and hurt them both.

"Keep your hands off me!" he shouted.

"Don't you touch those kids!" Yolanda shouted back, slapping him across the shoulders. Terrance kicked at her, she dodged, and then he tried to shove his way through. Yolanda pushed back and would not let him pass.

"Woman, don't make me teach you a lesson!" he sneered. His eyes were growing wild with desperation. Yolanda thought he might just do something scary, but he had gone too far for her.

"You put that TV back!" she ordered. "And *don't* call me 'woman.'"

"I bought the darn thing. I can do what I want with it."

"Like what? Sell it for drugs?"

Terrance couldn't continue the fight while holding the TV, so he backed up and set it down on the couch.

"What did you say to me?" he said, getting up in her face.

"You heard me!" she said, trying to prevent her voice from wavering. "You're not selling that TV for no drug money. That's one of the only nice things we have."

The boys started protesting again, but Terrance shouted them down. He turned back to his wife.

"Listen here—*woman.* You don't talk to me that way. Ever. Especially not in front of my own children. You'll show me *respect.*"

"Oh yeah?" Yolanda spat back. "Why don't you try acting respectable then, instead of like some punk, deadbeat street thug!"

Suddenly Terrance was pounding on Yolanda's shoulders and back and shouting all manner of accusations and insults at her. Michael started crying, and Tommy was crying in the kitchen. Tommy ran to the closet and returned with his father's bat and before anyone knew what was happening he'd struck Terrance square in the back.

Terrance shouted and stumbled backward. He rushed Tommy and slapped him to the floor then grabbed the bat and held it aloft.

"Did you just hit me? Huh? You little *fool!*" He swung the bat against Tommy's legs, and the boy let out a yelp. His brother began to shriek from across the room.

Tommy looked back at him with a gravity he'd never seen before in his son's eyes. "I'm not afraid of you," he said, and Terrance believed him.

"Well, we got a little man here? I guess I need to teach you something to fear!"

He raised the bat again, but Yolanda grabbed it from him and caught him across the chest with it.

"Y'all is crazy!" he screamed. "We a family! Y'all is crazy! I could break all your necks! Who do you think you are?"

"Tommy, get your sister. Michael, get your shoes. We're going." Yolanda said.

"Don't bother," Terrance said. "I'll go."

"Works for me."

Terrance hesitated a moment then marched to the couch to get the TV. Yolanda couldn't believe her eyes.

"You crack-head fool less than a man!" she shrieked and hit him again with the bat. Terrance roared with the pain and indignation. As if possessed, he lunged toward Yolanda and tried to wrestle the bat from her, but she would not release it. They pulled back and forth, until suddenly it slipped from her hands and Terrance went stumbling backward with it—sending it end-first through the television screen.

They all stared at the now-useless box of plastic, glass, and metal. Terrance let out something like a whimper then disappeared through the front door.

When he slammed the door shut behind him, it shook the wall and the couch up against the wall and the TV on the couch and the bat in the TV until the bat slid quietly out and clattered onto the floor.

12

Party Crasher

Music echoed up and down the street. It wasn't clear from where it emanated, but the occasional individual or couple carrying a bottle of wine or six-pack of beer around the back of a modest, single-story bungalow gave a good indication to the nosy neighbors peeking out their windows.

Paul and Lisa parked their nice car that just fit between a motorcycle and an even nicer car. They walked hand-in-hand toward the musical bungalow, Paul carrying some beer, Lisa carrying a bottle of wine.

The main party was around back, a squashed back yard typical in the city, with an apartment building rising in brown-orange brick along one side and another small house sitting modestly on the other.

A young man in tight pants and a patterned shirt burst out of a crowd of people as a couple entered through the gate.

"Hey, look who's finally here!" he shouted in greeting.

"Hey, Jason, happy birthday!" Lisa replied, giving him a hug and a kiss on the cheek.

"Paul, always good to see you," Jason said as the two men shook hands. Paul wished him a happy birthday, too, and Jason pointed him to some coolers full of drinks and a table with several bottles of liquor.

"I'll be right back, baby," said Paul, and he went to make them some margaritas.

Mila came running up too, and after she and Lisa hugged, she gave Jason an emphatic look.

"What's that about?" Lisa asked, beginning to suspect something was up.

"Well," Jason began, "I was just talking to Mila about a…potentially sensitive subject."

"About *me*?"

"No! No," said Jason. "It's about Yolanda."

"Oh, well, then I don't need to know," Lisa scoffed with a dismissive wave of her hand.

"You might want to know this," said Jason.

"Believe me, I don't."

"Lisa, come on," said Mila. "She's your sister-in-law. Show a little compassion."

Lisa scowled a little to be even gently importuned in this way.

"Yeah, okay, what is it?"

"She been acting different at the shop, y'know?" said Jason. "Taking long lunch breaks, coming back kinda happy and, I don't know, glowing, like…"

"Mila told me the other day she was scared of Terrance. Sounds like things are better now. That's a good thing, isn't it?"

"A good thing? You know Terrance hasn't changed his tune. So what you think she getting up to all that time?"

"I don't know, eating? Why don't you ask her yourself?"

"I did. She says she is swimming up at the gym or something."

"You want to tell me where the problem is in all this that you thought was so important to talk to me about?" Lisa watched for Paul or some other excuse to get out of the conversation.

"Look, honey," Jason said gently. "I think she's seeing somebody on the side."

"What?" Lisa was genuinely surprised and confused. "Yolanda? Cheating on Terrance? No way. That ain't her."

"It's as much as he deserves," Mila muttered.

"That may be, but she ain't like that," Lisa insisted.

"She ain't like someone who swims at the Y neither," Jason pointed out.

"Well, even so, what you want me to do about it?" Lisa said, growing impatient with the whole thing.

"I don't know: talk to her?" Mila said. "If your brother found out..."

"Look, I appreciate your concern, but this is not my problem, and it's *certainly* not your business," Lisa said. "Now I'm gonna find my husband and those margaritas."

She marched off and left the two friends feeling very unsatisfied.

The music continued to pound the air. People gathered in small circles to laugh and dance and argue about unimportant things. Lisa and Paul mingled and made small talk. At some point, Lisa found herself in a group with Mila talking about *The Sopranos*, and before long, the two were on good terms again—so long as Mila didn't mention Yolanda.

Paul's friend Rick showed up too, and the two men greeted each other with hearty slaps on the shoulder and went to get Rick a drink. If Paul was a bit of an outsider in this social circle, Rick could have been from another country. But Jason had met Rick many times at Lisa and Paul's house, and he'd invite him to things to keep Paul company.

Rick had served with Paul on the force, and both left around the same time. While Paul entered law school, Rick went off on his own as a private detective. Lawyers and private eyes weren't normal guests for Jason, but neither were marketing managers. That's what it was like growing up with Lisa, though. She did her own thing, brought her own energy.

In fact, that topic came up that evening, as such things do when old friends get together.

"What was, that, third grade, when you went as Little Orphan Annie for Halloween?" Mary was saying.

"Second," Lisa said amidst general laughter.

"Where did you come up with that stuff?" Brian chided.

"I remember you came to kindergarten Halloween as a ninja dog or something," Jason said.

"Hong Kong Phooey," Lisa said as they laughed some more. "That was a good show!"

"I didn't even know that *was* a show," said Ennis.

"What did you go as in high school, Scooby Doo?" said Brian.

"No, she was like, Charlie's Angels one year," Mary said.

"No, I was Diana Prince," Lisa said. Everyone looked at her as if they expected her to say more. "Wonder Woman's secret identity? Linda Carter?"

This drew incredulous laughter and shouts of "Get out of here!"

"Well, Jason actually came as Wonder Woman senior year!" Lisa complained.

"Yeah, but we expect that from Jason."

Meanwhile Rick and Paul were speaking seriously off in a corner of the yard.

"I saw the doctor the other day," Paul began. "He says I got this kidney disease."

"What?" Rick said.

"It's called ADPKD or something. It's like little cysts. They can do some stuff now, but I'm going to need a new kidney at some point."

"That's a bunch of crap," Rick whispered. He scrutinized Paul's red plastic cup.

"This is just water," Paul explained. "I'm off booze until we get this sorted."

"Wow, man. What did Lisa say?"

"I haven't told her yet."

"Why the heck not?"

Paul shrugged and shifted on his feet, sipped his drink.

"I don't know...it's complicated, you know?"

"You're going to have to tell her some time."

"I hate the idea of looking sick or weak in front of her," Paul said, his eyes on some point in the distance where maybe these things were happening to someone else.

"Man, she's your wife..." said Rick.

"I know, but lately... You know, she says she likes that I'm trying to make it as a lawyer, that we have this 'respectable middle-class lifestyle' and all, but sometimes...it's like there's some part of her that still wants a street tough, someone who's more protective and brags about her or something."

"What do you mean," Rick asked carefully, "like someone *blacker* or something?"

"In short. Someone more like Ennis over there. And maybe not a man on kidney medications hoping for a donor to show up."

Now they were both looking toward Lisa talking with her friends.

"Yeah, he's cut, isn't he?" Rick said. "But come on, this is Lisa. You said so, yourself."

"You know when her and her girlfriends go out, they like to wind up at his cocktail bar?"

"So you've said. He's a classy guy."

"Yeah, The Blue Train. And he likes to make their drinks himself."

"Oh."

"Yeah."

"What you gonna do?"

"I don't know yet."

The general festivities were interrupted by a small crew of people carrying a cake, alight with a dozen or more candles, from the house and beginning to sing "Happy Birthday."

"Look at Jason acting all surprised and flustered," Paul teased Lisa as he came up behind her and put his arm around her. "He's orchestrated every aspect of this party, and we all know it."

Lisa chuckled and said, "Yeah, he's a dramatic one."

Everyone cheered as Jason blew out his candles. Then he looked around with a demonstrative flourish, hung his shoulders, and announced that his wish hadn't come true because he wasn't five years younger and he didn't have a hot hunk of man on his arm.

Then there was some commotion by the side gate. Someone was pushing his way through and mumbling something. Then he was yelling at people, and they began to naturally clear a path for him.

"Is that Terrance?" Paul said. They were on the other end of the yard, but they could tell from the swagger and the voice—despite the drunkenness that made him wobble and slur.

"Hey, Brian, man," Terrance was saying. "Long time. Give a brotha ten dolla? Mary! Damn, girl, you fine as ever! Spot me a twenty? Alicia, my girl! You know if I didn't have a girl...well, but can I borrow a couple yards? Just for a week or so, you know, baby?"

He was working the crowd like a beggar on the L, moving on as soon as they broke eye contact and working his way around the yard.

"I need another drink," Lisa said just to say something. Paul grabbed her arm.

"Where you going?" he said through his teeth.

"To get another drink. I just said."

"Do something."

"Do what?" she said. "This ain't about me."

The rest of the crowd seemed to think it was very much about her, for they were all looking at her with the same look of importunity that Paul had.

"If you don't, *I* will," Paul said.

"If you go near that boy you can plan to spend the night here, because you're not coming home with me," she said, and shook herself free.

She picked her way on a path opposite to her brother's, but he soon spotted her by following the direction of everyone else's gaze.

"That my sister? Lisa?" he shouted. She kept walking, up the porch and to the table, where she poured herself some wine.

"Lisa! Somebody grab her a minute!" Terrance was yelling. "Lisa, I gots to talk to you! Look," he said to the crowd, "that girl ran me out of her house at gunpoint rather than give me a few bucks. How you like that for a sister?"

Lisa didn't even look at him, but with a cold, set face and a robotic motion walked inside the house and disappeared from view.

Rick tapped Paul's arm. "What he talking about?"

"I have no idea," said Paul, "but this isn't about to end well."

They started toward Terrance, who had come up on the porch. He was stopped by a couple large men who decided someone needed to step in. His face displayed rage and confusion when his sister shut the door on him.

"Where she going? Where she going?" he shouted.

"Come on, man, time to go home," one of the big guys said.

"That was my sister," Terrance persisted. "I'mma kill her is what!"

Then he yelled at the house, "What would Mama think, Lisa? What would Mama think?"

"C'mon, man, it's time to go," Rick said, coming up behind him. He grabbed Terrance's arm and tried to guide him toward the exit.

But Terrance wasn't having it. He yanked his arm away and wheeled around.

"You can keep your hands off of me, man!"

Rick got in close and tried to speak in a confidential tone. "Terrance, you're embarrassing yourself."

"I'm embarrassing *myself*?" Terrance shouted. He stood up tall and became grandiose as he addressed the whole party. "Y'all should see how this fool looks at my wife. My *wife*! I mean, I don't blame him, but it's some pathetic stuff. Embarrass myself, yeah right."

The stroke hit home; Rick threw his arms up and walked away in exaggerated frustration. But Rick had succeeded so far as to derail Terrance from his previous train of thought. Terrance stood in the middle of a small circle that had cleared for him and looked around in confusion, trying to get his fire back.

"Terrance, let me call you a cab," said Jason.

"Naw, naw, no cabs! Just…just give me a beer."

"I think you've had enough, don't you?" Jason said, but the two men had let him pass far enough that he was already at the coolers rummaging around in the ice. He pulled out a clear bottle with gold liquid, popped the top, and took a long pull from it.

"All I's axing for is a few bucks, man," he whimpered to no one in particular. "Y'all is some cold folks. Won't help a brotha out when he needs some dough."

It didn't really matter to whom he was speaking; it was clear to everyone he was defeated. As he began to walk away, he saw Paul and raised his arms in question. Paul shook his head and handed Terrance some bills from his wallet. At last Terrance left, feeling like it hadn't been a total waste of his time.

It took a while, of course, for the party to resume its former lightheartedness. After the initial stunned silence, there was a break-out of confused and shocked murmuring—what was that all about? How drunk was he? What did he think he was doing coming here like that? where did Lisa go, and why didn't she help her brother?

And then Jason proclaimed, "Hey, let's eat this cake, y'all!" and broke the spell of discomfort for good.

Paul found Lisa upstairs in a chair in a spare room.

"Hey, baby," she murmured and went back to sipping her drink and acting like nothing was wrong.

"Where the did you disappear to?" Paul said.

"Don't take a tone with me."

"What are you doing up here? What do you call that back there?"

Lisa wouldn't look him in the face, but she knew the steam was building in him.

"I *call* it getting some peace and quiet," she said to the wine-colored wall. "You're welcome to sit with me if you're not going to be all critical and in my business."

"Forget that," Paul spat. "You left us all out there with your brother storming around harassing everyone."

"So what? That boy is always embarrassing himself," she said.

"That ni—..." Paul caught himself. Lisa suddenly looked at him sidelong, eyebrows raised in warning. "That was your brother, okay? That wasn't cool, walking away like that."

Lisa was more than aware of all the stares that had followed her as she sauntered into the house. The expectation. The accusation. The pleading for help.

"What did you want me to do? I ain't in charge of him."

"It's not about being in charge of him, it's about being his sister and just…dealing with him."

"Paul, we've been over this. I don't 'deal' with that boy. He's his own man. He makes his own choices. I don't want nothing to do with him."

"Would you stop that? It doesn't work that way," Paul complained.

"It works that way with me," she said simply.

Lisa sipped at her drink and waited for Paul to either sit down and change the subject or leave, but he just sort of stood awkwardly by the door.

"What?" she sneered, waiting for some more lecturing.

"There's…something else," her husband stammered.

"What do you mean? What is it?"

Paul couldn't make eye contact with her as he told her, in a stammering, roundabout way, about his diagnosis. She put her drink down and rose to enfold him in her arms.

"Oh, baby, I had no idea!" she cooed. "What can we do? What can *I* do?"

"It's gonna be okay," Paul said. "He's got me on some meds for now, and I'll need to get on a transplant list…"

"I'll go to the doctor's first thing and see if I'm a match," she said, laying her head on his shoulder. He had received her embrace stiffly at first, and some part of him wanted to protest her offer, but he discovered he was weaker than he'd expected, needed her more than he had known, and he slowly melted into her arms and tried to hide the tears that forced their way to the surface like drops of blood.

13

TRO

Lisa sat in a row of blue plastic chairs in a windowless room holding a slip of paper with a number on it. She tried for all the world to look like she was there on mundane business, like she wasn't scared. She may have been more scared of not knowing just what to be scared of, but she could not deny that she was scared.

And feeling scared made her angry. It was her anger that made her call in sick to work and head to the courthouse instead. She waited patiently while number after number was called to the row of windows up front.

Paul's bombshell about his sickness had her still reeling. He'd always been such a strong person, such a strong presence in her life; it was unimaginable that he should be brought down by something so ordinary as a disease. And yet here they were.

Would she be there at the courthouse if he hadn't told her? Was it fear that he might not be able to protect her soon that made her pursue official measures? She could not decide. When the idea had occurred to her earlier, she wasn't sure how serious she was. If Terrance coming after her had made her feel unsafe in her own home, Paul being sick made her feel unsafe in her own skin, like a part of her was sick with him. There was nothing a temporary restraining order could do about that, yet there she was.

It was a couple hours before she made her way from the front windows to an intermediary desk and at last to a courtroom where she was to await her case. The judge was a middle-aged white man, which did not give her much comfort, though she believed in the justice of her position.

Unfortunately, things got off to a bad start. There were far more people than she'd imagined, for one thing. In fact, she had pictured the whole thing happening in a private room, not out here in front of twenty or thirty other people waiting their turn to be heard. Furthermore, it was late in the morning. The judge, deputy, and recorder conferred briefly about their lunch break and agreed to take one last case. That's when they called her.

The deputy invited her up to the podium, and the judge asked her to explain why she wanted the order. She stated simply and formally, "Your Honor, I'd like to take out a temporary restraining order against Terrance McNight, who came uninvited into my house and threatened to do me physical harm when I refused to give him any money."

The judge didn't find this particularly interesting or surprising. "What's your relationship to Mr. McNight?" he asked with a perfunctory air.

"He's, uh, my brother, Your Honor," Lisa answered.

"Your brother? And has he visited your home before?"

"Not often. A couple times, sure."

"And was he used to entering without an explicit invitation?"

"I, uh, I don't know," Lisa fumbled. "I mean, I guess he has a way of making himself comfortable. He's kind of a big personality. Goes wherever he pleases whether he's invited or not."

"And did you forbid him entry into your home this morning?" the judge asked.

"Well, uh, maybe not exactly. I certainly didn't make him feel welcome."

"But you didn't explicitly tell him not to enter? What were your exact words?"

"I think it was something like, 'Terrance, what the devil are you doing banging on my door?' and then he just waltzed right in."

"Mm-hm," the judge grunted, still cryptically expressionless. "And did you at any point tell him to *leave* your home?"

"Yes, Your Honor. I told him several times I wanted him out of my house."

"Okay, good. And at what point did he threaten you?"

"As he was leaving. He said if I made him leave, 'There's no going back. I won't forget this. It's life or death for me out there,' and then he said, 'It ain't gonna end well for you. You'll be sorry for this.'"

"I see. Has he ever said this kind of thing before?"

"No...I mean, not in this way. He can be dramatic and all, and he's probably said stuff like that, but this time was different."

"This time you believed he meant to do you physical harm?"

"Yes, Your Honor, I mean, maybe."

"Maybe?"

She could feel her normally collected self feeling flustered under the judge's inscrutable gaze. With each question, she felt she was somehow answering incorrectly, but she did not understand what formula or magic words she was supposed to speak to get what she wanted from this man.

"I don't know," she admitted. "At first it scared me. Then I thought maybe he just meant he'd go to our mother, get me in trouble with her—"

"Are you afraid your mother will hurt you?" the judge interrupted.

"No, no, nothing like that. She's verbally aggressive, but she never hit me since I was a kid."

"May I ask *why*, then you believe your brother will hurt you?"

"He's got a mean streak, you know? There was a look in his eyes. It didn't feel right."

The judge leaned forward with a sigh and folded his hands together.

"Please believe me when I say I understand your concern, Mrs. Drayton," he said, though his demeanor did nothing to support his meaning. "Please also understand that I need to know all the relevant facts in a case if I'm going to make the right ruling for you and for the people of the City of Chicago. Now, can you give me any evidence from your brother's past to support your fears? I see he's got a record here of petty theft and misdemeanors, but nothing violent."

"No, sir, but…"

"Yes?"

Lisa took a moment to scan the crowd behind her. The judge reminded her that she was to address him and no one else. There were things she hadn't even told Paul about, and now she realized she was going to have to tell the judge and everyone there if she was going to get the order.

"Well, Your Honor, this isn't easy for me to talk about…"

"I understand. I only need to know enough to know he's capable of what you're worried about."

"All right then. Well,…" and she began to talk.

She told him how in eighth grade Terrance beat up a boy who stood Lisa up for a school dance. She told him how Terrance had earned his stripes by roughing up customers who owed his boss money.

She told him about the time Terrance and his crew were in a fire fight with a rival crew from another hood because one of T's boys had made a pass at one of the other crew's sisters. How T had retaliated for the ambush by hanging one of the other crew's dogs from a basketball hoop in an alley.

There was more, but she hoped she'd said enough. She might as well have been standing naked before the whole courtroom as it was; she wasn't sure she could stand to say more.

"Mrs. Drayton," the judge began again, "all of that is reprehensible behavior, for sure, but it also suggests your brother has a strong sense of loyalty to friends and family. Are you sure you have reason to believe he means you harm and wasn't just speaking in anger?"

"No, Your Honor, this wasn't just anger. This was different, like I said."

"And what *exactly* made this different? What would make this fiercely loyal person want to hurt his own family?"

Now she felt both naked and very small. And foolish. A voice in her head—her mama's voice—told her to let it go. *What did you expect from some white judge? Ain't no justice for poor black folk like us.*

Another voice told her it was better to see it through. Success here would be a breakthrough for her, even if it meant humiliating herself for a moment.

"Well, Your Honor, I may have pushed him over the edge by my words and…and actions."

"Go on."

"You have to understand I was really scared. I didn't know if he was going to beat me up or not. I haven't seen him that desperate. So I ran upstairs and got my husband's gun…"

"You pointed a gun at him?" the judge asked for clarification's sake.

"Yes, Your Honor."

It was like she was on trial herself. The whole room seemed to turn against her, though she hadn't heard hardly a noise. The judge sat back in his chair and tapped a pen while he scanned her up and down in consideration of this new piece of evidence.

"And were you prepared to use this weapon to defend yourself?" the judge asked.

"I don't really know. My husband taught me how to shoot it, but I've never had to pull it on someone, before. Maybe I just wanted to make him take me seriously."

"Do you believe your brother had reason to believe you were prepared to shoot him with that gun?" The judge raised an eyebrow with this question.

"I…I think it surprised him. I think it offended him." Lisa wanted to believe that being completely honest was her best recourse, but somehow the truth felt weak before the judge's wooden dais. "He probably didn't think I would really use it," she muttered.

"And why did you wait until today to seek a restraining order?"

"I couldn't make up my mind about it, I guess. Then he showed up drunk at a party I was at this weekend—"

"You've seen him since the incident?"

"Just that once." She told him what had happened, which, when she said it, didn't sound like much.

The judge nodded thoughtfully and checked his watch. Then he leaned forward, crossed his arms on his desk, and said, "Mrs.

Drayton, I don't want to say you're being unreasonable here because your brother seems like a pretty rough character. But I am also getting the impression that you, shall we say, have learned how to handle yourself."

"I hope so, Your Honor, but it's not like that. That's not my world. I moved away, went to school. I'm an associate in an agency downtown…"

She wished she had some kind of work ID or some kind of passport showing all the upwardly mobile places she'd been.

"That may be true," the judge said with a shrug. "However, on the basis of the evidence you've presented, we have no reason to believe this is anything other than a family squabble that has acquired the appearance of violence because your family has a history of dealing with their problems through violence or the threat thereof."

Lisa couldn't keep from cocking her head in confusion. She wasn't sure she was hearing what she thought she was hearing.

"I have to deny your request at this time, but if you are prepared to sign a sworn affidavit regarding the things you've told us today, and if you can produce other evidence of Mr. McNight doing harm to you or to members of his immediate family, you may be able to get the ruling you're looking for. That is all for now. Good day."

14

Ennis's Shoulder

On the trip home, Lisa moved as if through water. She hadn't realized it at the time, but that had been her first real attempt to access the system since she'd graduated from college. And it rejected her.

What more did she have to do to prove she was a productive, harmless member of society? How long would she be punished for where she came from?

You still just a ghetto black gal to them, her mother's voice repeated.

She didn't want to go straight home. The veneer of normalcy, of having made it or at least making it work here in this city, in this country, it had grown suddenly thin. She didn't want to go home and have home feel like a lie, like someone else's home and someone else's life.

So she stopped in at The Blue Train, first. Ennis could see the world weighing her down when she came through his door.

"Work, the girls, your man, or *the* Man?" he asked.

"*The* Man," she said, laughing despite herself.

"Let me see what I can do." Ennis began to pull bottles from every which way. He was not a showy mixologist—no flourishes or juggling or spinning or any of that nonsense. He poured every bottle like it was hard liquor, and he handed it across the bar like it was a tonic specially prepared for your needs, whether you needed to come up, come down, keep going, or just forget for a while.

Whatever he handed her smelled strong and tasted stronger.

"Ennis, what the is this?"

"It's called a Horse Thief Cocktail. I found it in the first cocktail book written by an African-American man, the very dapper Mr. Tom Bullock. You're drinking one hundred years of black pride right there."

"Well, was he trying to congratulate the horse thief or kill him?" She took a careful sip. "It's actually good once you get used to it."

"Sometimes you've got to dive into the pain before you can come out of it," Ennis said. "You're gonna be all right."

At the bottom of that drink she found something like relief, something like acceptance, and something else quite akin to sadness. Ennis made her something else with Hennessey and a dash of wine and told her to take her time with that one.

"It's my brother, again, Ennis," she finally admitted.

"He come back around?"

"No, nothing like that. I tried to get a restraining order."

"And they didn't see what the problem was with a black man roughing up a black woman?"

She sighed into her drink.

"You got some peanuts or something back there?"

"Another, please."

"I'll give you a beer, but nothing stronger."

"Yeahalrigh'."

"Let him cool down. Or give him twenty or fifty bucks. It'll blow over eventually."

"Things don't 'blow over' with my family."

"They know how to hold a grudge, huh?"

"Brother man, we were born to a grudge and trained up in the way of the grudge."

"Oh, yeah? So what's yours?"

Lisa screwed up her face at the question.

"I'm not talk'n' bout me."

"Yeah, well, I am."

The warmth of her drink—Ennis had called it a Bamboo—encouraged her to take the question seriously.

"You want the God's honest truth?"

"I don't know a better kind."

"Everything you sees a grudge. From my impractical heels to my natural curls. It's all a big black middle finger to my mother."

"Wish I hadn't heard *that* story before. What's your version?"

"She loved Terrance more than me and let me know it. He was her precious boy. He could do no wrong. Meanwhile she was always telling me I wasn't pretty enough or was too bookish or too solitary. Nothing I did was the right thing. I always felt like she wanted me to play white folks' games and try to please them and be like them and all, but I didn't want any of that."

"Your mama's old school, you know. They had to play those games to get along."

"Don't mean I needed to."

"But you up and married a white guy anyway."

"You'd think she'd be happy, wouldn't you? But he was the wrong white guy. An ex-cop."

"He's a lawyer now, though."

"She believes you can take the cop off the streets, but you can't take the cop out of the man. He brought Terrance in, once, you know."

"Ah."

"They got to be friendly, at least, Terrance and Paul. But Mama never forgave him."

"She sounds like a bulldog, your mama."

"You don't know the half of it."

"Hey, we the only ones here."

Lisa sipped at her beer. Ennis was idly wiping down the bar and putting away glassware and cutting citrus fruit up in preparation for the evening.

"It was relentless, Ennis," she began softly. "From the time I got home until I could hide in my room after dinner. 'Why you dress like some black slut? Why you sittin' inside here when they's all those boys runnin' round outside? Look at those wild curls—people gonna think you from the African bush. You such a skinny little ghetto thing. You better learn to fix yourself up or you never gonna find no husband.'"

"Wow. That ain't right, my beautiful black sister."

"No, it ain't."

"I guess another beer won't hurt you none."

"You know she burnt me with an iron once?"

"What? On purpose?"

"I don't know. I never was sure. I was only in kindergarten, I remember, because it was summertime and I had to wear pants to school the next day and they chafed the burn."

"WOW, this is unbelievable. What happened?"

She told him about her mama's train of white boyfriends, each one, it seemed, skeevier than the last. How there was one, a man with his hair in a ponytail and a long mustache and always wore overalls. How he creeped her out, the way he looked at her. How once he even said, in her mother's presence, 'You know, you already pretty enough to freak, you are.'

Her mama had sense enough to kick him out for that remark, though it led to a loud fight and several threats of uncertain meaning to her five-year-old mind. When he was gone, her mother turned on her and slapped her upside the head. She continued slapping her and beating her shoulders and back as she berated her:

"You ain't so pretty! You too scrawny. Your hair too wild. That fool was just being nice to your ugly butt. Why you have to go giving him the eye for? What you have to go swishing your scrawny hips for? I bring a man round here I expect my own daughter to stay away from him, y'hear? Damn! He was just bein' nice, as it was. It don't mean nothin'. Don't go thinking it meant anything. It don't mean *nothin'*."

She hadn't known she'd done anything wrong. She had mostly tried to avoid that man. Now her mother was mad at her and it was somehow her fault, though she simultaneously believed it couldn't be her fault.

Her mother swung the ironing board off the wall and set the small end atop the dining table, the legs being broken. Lisa was still small enough to sit on the board while her mother moved the steaming iron back and forth and in tiny circles with a mysterious knowledge of how to turn a wrinkly mass into a shirt or pillowcase.

Little Lisa didn't know any better than to try to win back her mother's love, so she pushed a chair over and used it to climb up onto the ironing board, carrying a doll. She sat and babbled to her mother about the adventures the doll had had that day, the doll's problems with her friends, what kind of ice cream the doll liked, and so on.

Her mother, she could tell, was stewing, though she said nothing. Lisa was brushing the doll's hair when her mother set the iron down, perhaps harder than she was wont, but perhaps not so much harder, if at all, though why had she set it down facing her daughter and not away? It tipped. The pointed arch of its front landed flat against Lisa's bare thigh, just below the hem of her shorts.

The girl screamed like she'd been bit by the devil, and her mother shouted, "Sweet Jesus!" and immediately pulled the hot metal off of her and rushed her to the bathtub to run cold water over it.

That pain! It felt like it was inside of her, burning both down to the bone and up to the surface of her skin where it could scald anyone who might touch it. She cried there with her leg under the cold running water for five, maybe ten minutes, and though the cold dulled the initial sharpness, the burning inside faded only slightly, it seemed, or else she was simply not prepared to let go of the pain, for to let go, to calm down and have a moment to think about anything else would mean to think about why it had happened, and that might lead to the conclusion that her mother had done it on purpose.

But here was her mother crying and shushing and saying, "There, there," gently patting her leg dry, rubbing a thick layer of Vaseline on the wound and wrapping it with gauze, leading her to the couch to lie down.

"You got a scar?" Ennis asked when she had finished.

"Sure do. That's why you don't often see me in short shorts or skirts much to this day, though sometimes I will wear 'em."

"That's child abuse. She shoulda been locked up."

"I've never asked her about it. I still don't know if it wasn't an accident. What I remember more than the pain, though—and it burned for days afterward—was the way she cooed and shushed me while she was tending to me. For a few moments she was any other mother doing what she could to take care of her baby girl. It's still one of my few memories of any kind of tenderness from her."

"You mean, she finally treated you like she always treated Terrance?"

"Yeah, I guess that's it."

"But Terrance doesn't see it that way. He just sees you turning your back on them all."

"You sure know a lot for a guy who didn't go to college."

Ennis laughed. "I said I didn't *finish* college. But you run a bar like this, ask enough questions…you start to see how things work. What you gonna tell Paul?"

"That he was right: it was a waste of time. I'll try to convince him that T's too worried about finding some cash to actually do anything."

"But you don't believe that."

She finished off her beer.

"Nope."

When she was safely home—she shouldn't have driven; Ennis almost talked her out of it, but she could fake sober quite convincingly—she made herself some tea, sat down on the couch, and watched out the window. It was evening now. Paul would be home in about an hour.

Maybe the judge was right, though. Maybe she didn't have anything real to fear from Terrance. What would he really do? He pulls that "we all family" crap all the time, but he also means it. He'd always looked out for her in the past. Maybe he was just angry and embarrassed and would stay away rather than show his face around here again.

But some things she knew were true regardless of any other truths. He shouldn't have come over, and he shouldn't have touched her. He should have stayed far away from her and her quiet life.

15

It's "YAZ-meen"

As the day of her big presentation at work loomed, Lisa had less and less time to think about Terrance. She and Jazmin stayed later and later in the office compiling last minute data and double-checking figures and rewriting headlines and reorganizing slides.

It was grueling, in its way, and they both felt the weight of what was expected of them, the need to produce some brilliant insight into a nonwhite market segment, but Lisa fell into such work easily.

One night, after their tenth bathroom break, they stood together at the vanity mirror noticing the circles forming under their eyes.

"Jazmin, we can't do any more good here," Lisa announced. "The best thing we can do is go home and get some beauty rest."

"I can get behind that," said Jazmin, massaging her cheeks.

Lisa noticed a kind of questioning glance. "Was there something else?" she asked.

"Oh," said Jazmin, "it's no big deal, but it's *YAZ-meen*."

Lisa felt like she'd been caught with her fly down. "What's that?"

"My name," Jazmin said. "It's pronounced *YAZ-meen*, not *JAZZ-min*. No big deal." Jazmin shrugged in that cute and disarming way young women do, but Lisa's defenses were down.

"Oh my goodness!" she said. "You mean all this time we've all been mispronouncing your name? I am *so* embarrassed!"

"It's okay, really. It happens all the time."

111

"No, it's not okay," Lisa said. "It's bad enough everyone looks at us like exotic animals, they ought to at least get your name right—and me, especially!"

Jazmin smiled and shrugged, but Lisa thanked her for speaking up.

"You know," she said as they took the elevator to the ground floor, "I've really appreciated getting to know you, Jazmin." She gave some ironic emphasis to the correct pronunciation. "It's been nice to have a friend at work with everything going on at home."

"Oh, no," Jazmin said. "Trouble with Paul?"

"Not like that." She told her about his diagnosis. "The good news is that I'm an eligible donor."

"Oh, wow," said Jazmin, "but does that mean you'll have to miss work for the surgery?"

"Eventually. There are a few more steps to go through. It's complicated."

"I have to admit I've noticed it," Jazmin said. "At least, you've seemed a little weary lately."

They were in the front lobby now and had paused by a pillar before heading out into the warm spring night.

"That noticeable, huh?" said Lisa, dropping her shoulders. "Tell me your family isn't as perfect as you are."

"Uh, no," Jazmin scoffed. "First off, I'm far from perfect, but I appreciate the compliment. Second, my parents have never had a complete set of dishes because they are constantly throwing them at each other. One of my brothers is an abusive drunk and the other one is a college professor."

"What's wrong with being a college professor?"

"My parents emigrated from Iran. He was supposed to be a doctor."

They shared a pleasant laugh at this. It seemed like she'd been fighting with everybody, lately. To find a warm smile and listening ear in her colleague felt refreshing and reassuring. Jazmin appeared to her like an oasis or a quiet harbor. Not the end of her journey, but a safe, welcome stop along the way. Lisa looked into her new friend's eyes and took a leap of faith.

"Can I tell you something?" she asked Jazmin.

"Of course."

"There's some bad stuff been going on. With my brother. It's complicated, but let's just say he didn't like the way I kicked him out of my home when he came begging for money the other day. I have to tell you, I got scared. It's all so embarrassing, really. This isn't what I want my life to be about, but sometimes it just comes back to get me."

"Are you all right now?" Jazmin said with sympathetic eyes.

"I don't really know. Paul's po'ed, and I know he feels weak because of this kidney disease thing. I'm worried he'll try something. Do you know I even tried to get a restraining order on my own brother?"

"Wow. I had no idea all this was going on," Jazmin said. "I'm so sorry, honey."

"Thank you." Lisa wiped away a couple tears that managed to escape her eyes. "You work hard, try to make something of yourself. Try to do the right thing. Then something like this happens and you feel…"

"It's okay. It's okay."

Lisa closed her eyes, took some deep breaths, and collected herself. She was glad she'd unburdened herself to someone outside of the whole situation, but now she felt she did not want to say any more.

"I'm okay," she said. "Thank you for listening. I guess I needed to tell someone that."

"Well, I've got your back," Jazmin said, placing her hand gently on Lisa's arm.

"Thanks. Now, look," Lisa continued, leading them out the front doors, "let's talk about what comes next. We are so close, but this thing is still not ready. We both know how big this could be for both of us, but it has to be better than perfect. We have to stop worrying and get some good sleep. Avoid alcohol and sugar for the rest of the week, okay? And no sleep aids. Just your normal routine, maybe a little early, if you can. Read a book or a magazine to get your mind off work. Don't call me unless it's an emergency. Let's not even watch the TV so we don't have to see any ads. I don't want you to think about work from the time you leave this office till the time you get back in the door. Keep you fresh."

"Is that your pep talk?" Jazmin chided.

"No, that's my anti-anxiety talk. I'll come up with a pep talk for just before the meeting."

"All right. Let's get out of here."

They parted at the sidewalk in front of their building, and Jazmin went to her apartment somewhere along the Blue Line while Lisa returned to her nice house in her nice little neighborhood.

16

Crack House

Two men lounged on old clothes piled on older furniture in dark, smoky room. Little puffs of smoke whispered through their lips as they brought wonky cylinders of paper to their lips. Sunlight came in through the cracks in the broken blinds but wasn't up to the task of illuminating anything in the room.

All around them was the accumulated detritus of years of neglectful housekeeping: empty bags of chips and boxes of crackers, opened envelopes, old newspapers, pizza boxes, soda cans, and so many old shirts and socks you might expect a small battalion of soldiers to have left all their luggage behind.

Terrance sat on several ratty flannels and some sweatpants that had been on the chair when he got there. They felt like a buffer between him and whatever fluids stained the upholstery hidden beneath. He alternately took puffs from the pipe and sips from a large bottle of cheap beer.

His compatriot sat on the floor facing a coffee table that was almost invisible except for the small space the man had cleared with a wipe of his arm. There were several more bottles and a couple spent crack pipes on the table.

Terrance had been there a good hour already, not knowing what else to do with himself. Now that he was way up in the stratosphere, the swarm of thoughts and feelings in his head started coalescing around one pressing idea.

"T, you awfully thoughtful today," said the other guy.

Terrance leaned back and took a long swig of beer.

"Gary, man, I'm in some kind of trouble."

"Tell me about it. A black man can't *but* be in trouble 'round here, seems."

"I been trying to deal with it, y'know? But it ain't going well."

"S'a old story, bro," said Gary, taking a puff. "The oldest story."

"Ain't nobody want to help me, y'know? Just a twenty here, a hunnerd there, and I could get square."

"Bro's don't look out for each other like they used to."

"My own sister, Gary. Bro, my own sister threw me outta her house rather than help me get Big George off my back."

Gary glanced briefly at Terrance at the introduction of Big George's name. After a pause he opined, "It ain't right. Fambly gots to look out for fambly."

"You dogonright," Terrance murmured. "That witch is the coldest witch you ever seen, though, man. You know she pulled a piece on me?"

Terrance managed to present this as an example of the backwardness of the times, but Gary was visibly confused.

"Your sister did?" he said. "Man, what you do to her that she go for her piece? What she gonna do with it?"

"I didn't do squat. I invited her to my boy's birthday party, then I axed her for some money and she went ape-poop on me."

"Witch pull a piece she sho better be ready to use it."

"That's what I say too. Else you got to pay the consequences."

"There gone be consequences, sure."

They sat in silence for a time. Terrance was working himself up to something.

"Gary, I need your help, man."

"What you mean?"

"I mean with this problem. I need to make this problem go away."

Gary thought for a second.

"Big George?" he asked. Terrance stayed silent.

"Your *sister*?" Gary said. Terrance still didn't answer.

"Hey, I'm your boy, y'know, T, but you talking some serious stuff, either way."

"I know," Terrance said, still avoiding eye contact. "But I need to know if you got my back on this."

"Aw, man, T, this ain't a good time. I got to lay low for a while."

"What you mean? What happened?"

"You know that liquor store at that one corner?"

"That was you?"

"Yo, I drove by there the next day and they was loading an ATM onto some truck."

"You didn't have a mask?"

"I took it off when I got outside. The ATM was just around the corner, yo. They gonna see me walking away. They might have my face."

"Woe."

"You got that right. Ain't nobody gone see my black butt on the street for the foreseeable future."

Terrance was up and pacing. A nervous sweat formed on his face.

"Bro. Why you go mess up like that, boy?" he said as if it could help.

"Freak you. It was an honest mistake."

"Freak. Freak!" Terrance raged. He kicked the wall and heard the cheap wainscoting crack. He threw his arms around as if swatting invisible gnats.

"Well, look, man. You got a few bucks then?"

"Not like you need."

Terrance sat back down and looked from joint to pipe and back again. He picked up the joint, took a long suck on it, and let the warm wave take him to Never-Never Land, to the Emerald City.

17

Paul Goes on the Hunt

Paul was stewing. He'd always been a man of action; that's why police work had suited him. He obsessed over the image of Terrance roughing up Lisa, scaring her, and him nowhere in sight to protect his own wife. He'd find his mind drifting onto the subject during meetings, or he'd wake up from a daze to realize he'd been staring blankly at his computer screen.

Lisa had suggested he pursue law because he often complained about how justice actually looked for the people on the street. Sometimes the wrong people got brought in and were not treated well before the mistake was discovered. Or sometimes they got the wrong people but the sentences came down harder than seemed right. Well now here he was doing the law thing, and what he lacked in attention to detail he made up for with passion and a strong sense of justice and purpose. But it was a lot of sitting and reading.

Lisa had insisted on being tested as a donor. When the first test came back with a strong probability of a match, she hugged him and cried with excitement, but he could only feel a sense of heaviness.

Lisa had told him to leave Terrance to her, to stay put and not try to fix things. It was her family, after all; she knew how to handle them. So each night he would watch as she got into bed and think about how someone had made this strong, bright, lovely woman feel weak and afraid—and he was not supposed to do anything about it?

Then she told him about her embarrassing ordeal at court and being denied a TRO. He hadn't even known she was going to court. And here was another case of someone making his wife feel small. Another judge or another day, and things may have gone differently, but even still. His own wife felt unsafe, and instead of relying on him, she'd gone to the authorities.

Then she'd gone to Ennis. Ennis was a good man—there was no doubting that—but he shouldn't have been first on the list of confidants.

Seem like Lisa know what all I *should and shouldn't be doing but don't know what* she *should and shouldn't be doing,* he thought in the voice he sometimes used in his head when he wanted to feel more like he belonged to Lisa's world. *Seem like maybe she needs to learn herself a lesson.*

He laughed at his own machismo, but he also knew something ugly was brewing inside and he was worried it would come out one way or the other. Terrance was at the root of it, and it was better for Terrance to get the brunt of this force than for it to come out in some unexpected way on Lisa.

If she couldn't trust her family or the authorities to protect her, who else but her husband, anyway? Or so was his thinking by the end of the day. He called Rick.

"You sure this is a good idea?" Rick asked him. "If we get in any trouble, Lisa will freak. And your bosses sure as hell are gonna freak."

"We're not going to do anything to draw attention," Paul said. "I just need Terrance to know what he can and can't be doing out there. I'll come get you after dinner."

Paul stopped home and tried to be present for his wife despite his impatience to be moving. He gave her a long hug when he came in the door then helped with the last preparations for dinner. He listened with compassion to her stories about work and her upcoming presentation.

While Lisa was cleaning up after dinner, he walked upstairs and found his bat where it stood by his side of the bed. He opened their window and tossed it carefully into the bushes that ran along the front of the house. Then he returned downstairs, told his wife he was going to meet Rick for a drink. She looked a little surprised, but shrugged and told him to have fun, said maybe she'd go down to Ennis's. He kissed her goodbye and left through the front door.

He retrieved the bat and threw it in the trunk of the car. For a moment he wondered if he should get a gun from Rick, but he wanted to keep things at the level of bruises and hard words. He wasn't sure how desperate Terrance was, but he didn't believe it would escalate to guns. It wasn't his style.

Next stop was Rick's place. His friend walked out the door as soon as he pulled up to the curb.

"Do you have your...?" Paul asked.

"Yep," said Rick, patting his jacket pocket.

"All right, but let's try not to need it. And not for Terrance. It's his gangsta wannabe punk crew I'm more worried about."

"If he's even with his crew."

"Let's hope."

They drove to Terrance's house and parked right out front. Paul left the bat in the trunk, and they walked straight up to the door and knocked several times. An attractive young woman came to the door in wide-legged pants and a close-fitting cotton top. Yolanda wasn't as beautiful as Lisa, but she was still too much woman for Terrance. She didn't seem happy to see Paul.

"What you doing here?" she said when she recognized him.

"Hey, Yolanda, sorry to bother you," Paul said as casually as he could. "How's everything going? How are the kids?"

Yolanda peeked around behind him and saw Rick.

"What he doing here? What you want?"

"I was hoping to talk to T. Is he around?"

Yolanda pursed her lips with distaste and looked Paul up and down for the third time. "This about him coming round your house to push his sister around?" she said.

"I'm surprised he said anything to you about it. Or at least about his part in it."

"The girls were talking down at the beauty shop," she said. Her voice was firm, but her expression said *This man never causes me nothing but trouble.*

"That's where you've been all day?" Paul asked.

"I just got home from taking the kids to McDonald's, not that it's any of your business."

"They talk about anything else at the beauty shop?"

"Say *she* got rough with *him*. Drew down on him."

"I guess that tells you how scared she was. Yolanda, I'm taking this seriously. I know they're family, but I can't let him threaten her like that. I need to talk to him."

"Well, she right to be scared," Yolanda said in a low, hard voice. "I never seen T so desperate. He tried to sell the TV right out from under the kids' nose the other day."

"Tell me where to find him."

"T would kill me if he even *heard about* me talking to you now," she said.

"I can't help that, but I'm not out to get you in trouble. How could you live with yourself if he hurts his sister? Or worse?"

Part of her wanted to reject the premise of the question, but it wasn't a strong part of her, and she relented on the tough act. Nonetheless, she had to acknowledge she didn't know where Terrance was. She gave Paul a couple addresses where he might be and suggested they start at his mother's house.

"He go by there sometimes after dinner to check in on her, drink a beer or something."

"I really don't want to go up there," Paul said, looking at a small house from out the car window.

"Because if he's in there it means *she*'ll be in there?"

"Yep."

"Do or die, brother," Rick sang.

"*That* is not exactly funny in this situation. Here I go."

"She" was Joyce McNight, Terrance and Lisa's mother. Paul had only met her a handful of times—and never at Lisa's instigation. He knew her as an abrasive, spiteful, angry woman who openly expressed her disapproval of their marriage.

The house was only a couple blocks from Terrance's and of much the same Chicago-bungalow construction. It differed, however, in that it was a complete shambles. One might almost think it uninhabited by the state of decay and vegetal growth in and around it. None of the houses on the block was in saleable shape, but at least folks swept their porches and mowed their lawns. The lack of even these minimal signs of care made the poor little house appear an orphan, a vagrant hungry for a crust of bread or a kind word.

Paul didn't even think about bringing the bat; Joyce wouldn't so much as open the door to him if he did. As it was, he had Rick wait down on the sidewalk rather than let Joyce find two white men at her door.

He hesitated a moment at her door then hit the bell. There was no answer, just the sudden shrill barking of what could have been a dozen or more small dogs. He hit the bell again, and the dogs renewed the urgency of their barking. As if from somewhere far away, a voice cut through the ruckus: "Who the devil ringing my bell?"

Paul cocked his ear toward the door to try to catch the direction of the voice. He briefly looked up and down to locate it in the basement or upper floor.

"Joyce? It's Paul. Drayton. Where are you?"

"What you want? Why you come round here?" came the voice, sharper but no nearer. He could hear the dogs skittering around the door and front windows, banging into the glass and nearby furniture. Something metallic fell to the floor with a crash like dull lightning.

"I need to talk to you," Paul called back, still scanning the house in search of his interlocutor. Her voice floated around him, behind and before, above and below. "Are you in there? Can you come out?"

He heard the voice mumbling, upstairs, he thought, in the northwest corner, only then he heard cursing that seemed to come from the basement in the southeast corner. He gave Rick a confused look, and Rick looked equally as lost.

"Go the freak away!" the voice shouted suddenly from somewhere near enough to make Paul jump.

"Dammit, Joyce, just open up! It's about Terrance!"

After a moment's hesitation, the voice, from still a new direction, told him to meet her around back.

Paul descended the porch steps and indicated to Rick that he should stay out front. He rounded the house and followed the narrow cement walk to the back gate. Before he could open it, three tiny dogs—black and white Boston terriers and a dirty mop of a Yorkshire—ran up to it and tried to climb it with their paws and teeth, barking all the while even when their mouths appeared full of metal fencing. Joyce came up from behind.

"That's far enough," she said—to Paul, not the dogs. "What you want with me? Why you come round here with us common folk for?"

Joyce was short and getting wiry as she aged, but she still had remnants of the attractive face and curves that had gotten her into trouble in her youth. Long decades of fighting everyone and everything to get her small sliver of the American Dream had made her wary and suspicious, sometimes intolerably so.

"Quiet down now!" she yapped at her dogs. She brushed them away with her foot, but they immediately returned to the gate and only decreased the frequency of their barks.

"What you got to say about Terrance? Is Lisa with you?" she snapped.

"No, Lisa doesn't even know I'm here," Paul acknowledged. "But I was hoping you knew where Terrance might be. I'd like to have a word with him."

"With *him*? You should be having words with your *wife*! Do you know what that little witch did to him?"

"Joyce, I don't want to get into it with you right now, I—"

"Oh! You don't want to 'get into it right now!' You got some big important things to do. Fancy lawyer boy doesn't want to hang around the hood too long and get his fingers dirty. Well, you best leave my Terrance alone, 'cause he like to give you a black eye before he let you 'have a word' with him."

Paul was never one to back down from a good fight, especially where his dignity was concerned, but he tried to stay focused on Lisa.

"Joyce, this is serious. Terrance threatened her. She's scared, and I'm not going to have nobody, no matter who it is, come round my house and scaring my wife."

"Scared of what? Terrance? He's her brother—what he gonna do? You got your panties all in a twist over some siblings having a little spat. You don't know nothing about it."

"I know Lisa tried to get a restraining order."

"She what? That crazy witch! Against her own brother? I cannot believe my ears. That girl has lost her everlasting mind."

Joyce was acting angry, but Paul could see he'd frightened her. She was scared for the very reason that had motivated Lisa to do it: it wasn't how things were done in the hood.

"But she pulled a *gun* on him! *He* should get a restrainiment order on *her*! What's going to happen to him?"

"Nothing, Joyce. Her request was denied. Apparently, the judge agreed with you that it was just siblings having a spat."

"Well, we both know why he thought *that*," she spat, but the spite was reflexive and her voice was growing quieter as she grew suddenly thoughtful. He gave her a moment to process—and himself a moment to calm down from the verbal assault.

"Look," he began, "I know you don't like me"—she scowled when he said this—"but I wouldn't be here if I didn't think it was serious. I need to find T and talk him down from doing anything stupid or hurting someone."

"Hurting someone?" she mumbled. "Hurt someone? That girl don't give us a second thought unless it's to talk a load of stuff about us, and her brother goes to ask her for some money and she chases him out of her big fancy house with a gun—chased *my baby* with a gun—and you're worried that *she's* gonna get hurt?"

"Joyce, I don't want to fight with you…" Paul seethed.

"Don't you go threatening me," Joyce hissed. He'd never heard her talk in anything other than growls and hisses. "You don't scare me, none. You know why a black girl marries a white boy? Because she know he not man enough to keep her in line."

"What?"

"He bring home the money and she tell him how to spend it," Joyce said, triumphing over him.

"This is absurd. Where's Terrance?"

"You know what she tole me before you got married?"

"She hasn't talked to you in years," Paul replied, but there was a challenging look in Joyce's eyes that undercut his confidence in his own words. Even as he said them, Joyce broke out in a knowing smile.

"Oh, so she didn't tell you, huh? She didn't tell you about our little conver-*say*-tion? Oh, yes, honey. You can bet I spoke to my daughter before she married herself off to a white man. I been with enough white men to know what to watch for, and I had a motherly duty to warn her, much good as it did."

"What are you talking about, Joyce? Is there a point to this?" Paul hoped there wasn't.

"I told her not to look for no Prince Charming, see. And she tole me you wasn't no Prince Charming, you was somebody she could take care of."

He couldn't hide the way her words disarmed him, and he hated himself for it and her for the way she fed off of it.

"You barely more than a nice pet, my boy," Joyce said as if she'd knifed him in the ribs.

"You're lying," Paul said, hoping to make it true. "You're a sad old woman. I feel sorry for you."

Joyce exploded. "Get the freak off my property!"

But Paul was finding his feet again—and a target for the dark force inside him.

"All the stuff that's happened to your daughter—all the stuff that *you* put her through," he snapped. "The least you can do is help me protect her, but no, you're too freaking jealous of her to act like her mother! You've always been jealous of her! It's pathetic."

Two quick hits of a car horn sounded from the street. *Rick*, Paul thought.

"Jealous of my own daughter?" Joyce was saying. "You've got to be smoking some straight up freaked crack to believe that."

"I believe that's Terrance's drug of choice," Paul returned.

"Man, you best get *off* my *property* before I go get a gun of my own. Don't you go talking stuff about my boy doing drugs round here."

"Freak it, I'll go," said Paul. "But if his own mother can't admit to what's going on, things are not going to end well for Terrance."

"Get your white butt out of here, and tell that witch you married to keep the freak away from us!"

The horn sounded again, and Paul pulled himself away. Rick was standing by the driver's side door waiting for him.

"Didn't want to be rude, but I heard Joyce yelling and was worried you'd say something stupid."

"Too late," said Paul. "You should have just come knock me out with the bat."

"Next time. Where to now?"

18

Showdown

They spent a little time roaming the blocks of the neighborhood looking for familiar faces or just anyone hanging out. A couple times Paul called out the window to someone standing on the corner, but no one could—or would—help him. One guy, after Paul massaged the truth a bit and said he was just worried his brother-in-law was in trouble but couldn't reach him by phone, told him to go look around Martin's house a couple blocks over.

They guessed which house was Martin's by the number of guys hanging out on the front porch looking very relaxed.

Rick eased the car into a spot across the street. They both got out of the car slowly, casually, as if they could be going anywhere or nowhere. Rick popped the trunk but left it just slightly ajar. He came around to the passenger side and leaned back against the vehicle, arms folded. Paul meandered in a long arc toward the house, like a shark fixing to surprise a school of piranhas.

Of course, he wasn't going to surprise anyone. The men on the porch noticed two white guys in their neighborhood right away, and while some of them kept chatting as if nothing was up, the one sitting at the top of the steps carefully watched Paul from the moment he exited the car. As Paul crossed the lawn on his indirect arc, the man jerked his chin toward him and said, "Yo, yo, whattup?"

Paul met the man's eyes long enough to jerk his chin back in greeting then looked off any which way. During his whole conversation with them, he never locked eyes for more than a second or two but always acted almost uninterested in his own words and like he was preparing to walk off at any moment.

"Hey, how's it going? I was hoping you fellas might be able to help me," Paul said.

The guys on the porch had gone quiet and were all watching Paul now. They chuckled a little at the idea that they had anything of use to him—or that they'd be willing to give it to him if they did.

"Oh yeah?" said Crispy, the man on the stairs. "Well, we don't know nothing about nothing, so, y'know, you wasting your time around here."

"You're Terrance McNight's crew, aren't you?" Paul said, and he could tell from their subtle reactions that they were. "He's my brother-in-law."

This definitely got their attention, though it would be a stretch to say they were warming up to him.

"Yeah, he told us about you," said Eddie, who at least was smiling. "Who your friend?"

Paul told them Rick was driving him around since his wife had their car.

"Ain't you used to be a cop?" said Chris C.

"This was my beat, yeah. Seems like a long time ago, though."

"What you doing now?" Martin asked him. Martin was such a large dude, physically and psychologically, that when he leaned forward Paul reflexively took a step back to give him more room.

Paul chuckled to himself. "Well, I'm a lawyer—"

They immediately set off whooping and hollering and laughing at him.

"Now hold on, guys," Paul broke in, trying to laugh along. "I've crossed over. I'm in criminal defense now. I have seen too many guys get a bum rap, and I'm trying to do something about it, okay?"

"Yeah, you a regular Robin Hood, I'm sure," Martin scoffed. His chair creaked and groaned as he sat back in it, and the other guys enjoyed a brief laugh.

"Just one man trying to do right. You know where T is, or what, fellas?"

"Lemme ax you something," said Crispy from the stairs. "If you such a good guy, how come T don't like you none?"

"Shuck, you guys know Terrance. He's got his own way with things. I can't tell you why he likes something or someone or doesn't like them."

They seemed to reluctantly agree to this.

"Freak it, *I* don't like *him* sometimes," he added, and he knew by their smiles he was impressing them. "But look, he's family, so if he's in trouble I want to help."

They conferred amongst themselves in grunts and mumbled words, then they gave him an intersection where they knew he often made deals. Paul thanked them, then as he was leaving threw out, as if an afterthought, "Hey, is he still carrying that stupif ol' pea-shooter of his?"

"Naw, man, not lately," Eddie said with bemusement. "Cops been giving him trouble, and he can't be found carrying or they'll pick him up."

"Freaking cops, right?" Paul said with a shoulder shrug. They laughed some more and cheered him, half-mockingly, half in earnest, as he walked back to the car.

"That went better than I expected," said Rick. "You're not bad at this."

"It's been a while, though," Paul said. "My heart is pounding."

"What were they gonna do?"

"I don't know, but there was enough of them that they'd probably get away with it if they did…"

Rick discreetly pushed the trunk closed as he walked around the car and got back behind the wheel. They drove a couple blocks west, then a few more north, toward an alley that ran behind a shopping center.

It was dark now. As they pulled up to the corner in question, Paul could see a couple guys hanging out there under the streetlight, but he could tell neither was Terrance. That wasn't right, but they looked young, wannabes maybe, who were going to have to learn the life the hard way.

Rick pulled over, but as Paul got out of the passenger side the guys freighted and started running. Rick popped the trunk, Paul grabbed the bat, and they gave chase.

The guys knew the neighborhood, but they were too big to move fast, so they didn't have time to dodge into a yard or house or wherever. Rick caught one of them and shoved him against the chain-link fence that ran behind the shopping center. Paul managed to grab the other one, but as he did the guy swerved, reaching for his back. Paul didn't waste time wondering what he was reaching for, but stopped and swung around, bringing the bat up as he did. He knocked a small pistol right out of the guy's hand. He cursed and fell to one knee while the gun slid across the alley.

"This guy's clean!" Rick yelled from about a dozen feet behind. He had frisked the guy then sucker-punched him in the stomach and started pounding on him until he hit the ground. When Paul looked over, Rick was kicking the guy in the gut.

"Whoa, Rick!" Paul called, trying not to sound surprised. "Let's give ourselves something to work up to, at least."

Paul pointed the bat at his guy, who was moaning over his hand.

"Look, I'm not here to rough you up," he said, unconscious of any irony. "I'm looking for Terrance McNight. That's his corner. Where is he?"

"Freak you, man! We on Big George's crew, and he ain't gonna like you messing with us."

"Bull crap. Big George's crew doesn't work this neighborhood. Now either of you know where Terrance is, or you're too stupid to know to keep off his corner, and either way, he just might appreciate me working you over with this bat some more."

Paul emphasized this notion by jabbing the guy in the ribs. Not enough to break anything, but possibly to leave a bruise.

"Shuck, man!" said the guy. "Uh, black man can't stand around a corner no more without some wonnabe tough guy busting his butt over it."

"Your butt, your legs, your face. I'm considering my options."

"Man, freak you," the guy shouted, but his tone betrayed his defeat. "Terrance over by the old shoe factory building. Been hanging out there Tuesdays for some reason."

Paul looked at Rick.

"Let's go," Rick said.

Rick ran the car up onto the curb and Paul jumped out with bat already in hand. Terrance recoiled then took off running when he saw the look on Paul's face.

Terrance ran down an alley beside the old factory then rounded to the rear of the building. When Paul came around the corner, he heard a door falling shut about thirty feet away. He entered the building more cautiously, preparing for a possible ambush, but he could hear footsteps running away from him still.

He ran down a hallway in the direction of the footsteps, his blood up, anticipating the showdown. The hallways would have been pitch black, but light struggled in through the large office windows along the outer wall, and he could hear that Terrance was some ways ahead of him.

The hall turned at the corner and seemed to stretch interminably into the distance. Paul guessed that Terrance hadn't actually gone all the way down. Instead, he stopped at a set of double doors about midway. Through their windows he could see what must have been the actual factory floor, an open hall occupied by a few strange machines that didn't get sold off and were left to go gray with dust and cobwebs.

Paul kicked open one of the doors, and instantly Terrance came round and swung an iron bar at him. He wasn't near enough to connect, but with a quick jump Paul closed the distance and jabbed Terrance in the gut with the end of the bat. Terrance stumbled backward and disappeared into deep shadows in the middle of the factory floor. Paul walked through the doors and stood up tall and straight in a patch of blue moonlight.

"I'm not here to hurt you, Terrance," he said, loudly but not yelling. "But I won't say I wouldn't enjoy it if it comes to that."

"Fool, why you jump out of a car with a bat then?" Terrance shrieked from the black shadows.

"Because I don't know how reasonable you're going to be," said Paul.

Paul could just distinguish Terrance's panting from his own. He faced the direction of the shadows he thought Terrance's voice came from.

"You've gone too far, T," Paul continued. "You come in my house and attack my wife?"

"She holding out on me, yo," said Terrance. "She my sister, and she won't help me. I got kids to feed, man!"

Paul hadn't had many interactions with his brother-in-law, but he'd never heard him quite like this. Desperate, scared. More like a treed squirrel than his usual peacock self.

"Look, you should have come to me then," he told him. "What the devil are you thinking going after her like that?"

"Man, freak you, and freak her! I ain't axing you for nothing. And I can't forgive Lisa for what she done to me. Now my momma call me and tell me Lisa trying to get a restraining order on me. On *me*? Her own brother? Freak you both. I got nothing else to say to you."

There was a wildness and rage in his voice that told Paul he couldn't let it go at that.

"I still got lots of friends on the force, T, and I can have them make it very difficult for you to do what you do, but if you come after my wife, you'll have me to answer to, and I may just forget that we're related."

Terrance was spitting mad now, and Paul could hear his footsteps pacing back and forth maybe twelve feet in front of him. "Yeah, you a real cowboy, you white freak. Get your posse together and lynch a poor black man and think yourself a freaking hero. I told Lisa you weren't enough man for her...."

"Hey, forget you!"

"Forget you right back, idiot. You think you can keep a black woman happy? Stupid."

"You talk big for a guy whose wife is stepping out on him," Paul snapped.

"What you talking 'bout?"

"The man's always the last one to know, isn't he? I can only imagine what they're saying at the beauty parlor."

Terrance hesitated.

"I'll deal with *her* later. You gonna help a brother out or am I have to deal with you, too?"

"Naw, you've gone too far this time, T. You're done. Cut off. Don't you show your face around my house or my wife no more."

"Man," Terrance laughed. "Black witches, huh? Get a brother *all* messed up till he don't know his head from his elbow. How much you wanna bet some big black freak is giving it to both our women? I bet it's that big elephant Ennis too."

"All right, we're done here, you ignorant fool." Paul was shouting without thinking. He lunged forward and swung the bat. He heard the rustle of Terrance's jacket as he dodged out of the way.

"Yes, yes," said Terrance, briefly emerging into a shaft of light before disappearing again into the shadows. "That's a sensitive subject, ain't it? Look, man, I get it. And here you are running around town after me while your own wife got a booty call only blocks away."

"Don't talk about her that way," Paul growled, swinging again. They circled each other in the dark.

"Tell me something," Terrance said. "How sad she look when you said you was going out tonight?" He was growing more confident with the quaver in Paul's voice. "Maybe you best get your butt home and check on your woman."

"Not before I beat yours," said Paul. He lunged at Terrance's voice and caught a piece of his arm.

"Shucks, man," Terrance whined. "You know what? You all is dead to me now anyway, y'hear? You just cogs in a machine that's gotta be blown up."

"And what?" Paul shouted, his voice growing hoarse. "You're gonna blow it up, T? You're some kind of crusader now?"

He took another swing, but Terrance was not there.

"If you weren't so damn stupid you'd've let me help you get a real job years ago and maybe then you wouldn't be such a mess-up all the time," Paul said.

Terrance stepped forward so that his face came into the moonlight. His eyes were wide and his head twitched funny. Paul even took a step back to brace himself. Terrance grabbed the bar with both hands and started walking toward him; Paul gripped his bat and prepared to swing again.

But suddenly he felt the return of the excruciating pain in his gut. He put a hand to his side and fell to one knee. Terrance stopped about six feet away, looking confused and even a little scared.

"What the devil going on? What's wrong with you?" Terrance shouted.

Just then Rick appeared at the double doors. He noted Paul on the ground, Terrance with the bar, and drew his gun.

"Back off, fool!" he shouted. He was surprised to see fear in Terrance's face—not of the gun but of whatever had happened to Paul.

"Yo, man, something's wrong," said Terrance.

Rick shuffled forward holding the gun straight out with both hands.

"Just drop the bar and back away! Now!"

Terrance threw the bar away and stepped back into the shadow.

"Hey, man, I didn't touch him," came his voice from the dark. "He just fell over. I think he need a ambulance, man."

Rick lowered the gun and knelt beside Paul.

"Shucks."

Terrance made a wide arc around them and slipped out the door.

19

A Man with a Bat

"Hang on, Paul. I'm calling 911," Rick said. "Just stay with me."

"No!" Paul groaned. "No ambulances. No hospital. It's going away."

He was, indeed, beginning to relax and uncurl, but he was sweating and panting heavily and looked pale.

"It's going away now. It'll be all right."

"I don't like it," said Rick. Let me take you to the ER at least."

"It'll be fine. It always goes away. Give me a minute and we'll get going."

He lay there on the floor catching his breath and recovering his equilibrium. Rick sat down against a wall and tried not to look as worried and uncertain as he felt. They lay there for several minutes in the cool, dark silence.

"Where's Terrance?" Paul asked when he felt more himself.

"He took off," Rick told him. "Seemed pretty scared. Think he got the message?"

"I don't know. My falling down probably freaked him out more than chasing him with a bat did, though." He tried to laugh, but it came out wheezy. "Help me up."

Rick crawled over to him and carefully helped him to sitting. They stayed that way for some time, then Rick helped him to stand and they shuffled out of the building. Rick supported his friend all the way to the car then slid him into the passenger seat.

"Get me home," said Paul.

"You sure about this?" he said. "Let's just go to the hospital."

"No, you have to get me home. T knows I'm down. If he was going to do anything, it'd be now."

"It's possible," said Rick. "Should we call Lisa?"

"I don't think we'll need to. Yolanda said she'd just gotten home with the kids, which means T will have to go home to get the car. We've lost some time, but we should be able to beat him."

"Let's go then."

"Try not to get stopped," Paul said as Rick peeled out of the alley. He looked at his watch impatiently.

"It's not good, man," Paul said after a block or two.

"Your kidney thing?" Rick asked.

"How can I protect my wife if I curl up in a ball in the middle of things?"

"Man, it's not your fault," Rick said. "You just have to deal with this thing, take it seriously, and get the help you need. Then you'll be back in business."

"It ain't that simple, man. I know what I have to do if I just want to survive this, but I don't know how I can ever recover in Lisa's eyes."

"Dammit, Paul," Rick said and hit the steering wheel. "You been like this ever since you guys were going out. She wouldn't have married you if she didn't think you were man enough, all right?"

It felt like the last word, but then, his eyes still closed and leaning his head against the seat, Paul added, "You know where she was tonight?"

Rick's brow creased. "You don't mean…?"

"Yep. Watching Mr. Beefcake Cocktails shaking her up something special."

"Okay, well, that doesn't sound great, I'll give you that. But she wouldn't…?"

"I honestly don't know. I mean, you may be right about the street still being in her. Why did Terrance bring it up? Anything's possible."

"Do you want me to…I don't know, look into it?"

Paul hadn't thought of it in such crass terms. Just the idea of suspecting his wife enough to put a PI on her made his guts twist up.

"I don't know what I'd do if it was true, man," he said. "There's still some of the street in me, too, you know."

Rick drove around Paul's block once then through the alley before finally pulling up to the front of Paul's house. "Look, are you sure you're all right? Do you need help getting inside?"

Paul took several deep breaths and still looked pale, but he refused any help.

"Paul, I don't like the look in your eyes," Rick said. "You still look like you want to fight someone."

"If someone needs fighting."

"We didn't see T's car. I think everything's all right."

Paul looked toward the bedroom windows.

"Is it?" he said and got out of the car.

Rick watched in the mirror as Paul retrieved the bat from the trunk then made sure his friend got inside his house safely. The front hall light went on, then it and the porch light both went off, and Rick pulled away.

In the blue light of the moon, a beautiful woman slept quietly, if not quite peacefully. She had blankets pulled up to her chin as if for protection, as if to hide from the bad stuff of the day.

But bad stuff has a way of finding you. A man's shape appeared in the doorway, holding a bat. He stepped into the room and stood over the woman sleeping there, breathing heavily.

He swung the bat casually by his leg, feeling its weight. It hit the side table with a knock loud enough to wake the woman. She jumped to the other side of the bed before she'd even had time to turn around and see who it was.

The man didn't move, only stood there watching her as she came to her senses.

"Oh, Paul," Lisa said. "I thought for a minute you was…"

She cut herself off abruptly, awkwardly. She could see the anger in the way he stood.

"What?" Paul said with forced breath. "Say it."

"What happened to you? Are you all right?" she said. "You were gone so long."

"Don't dodge me, baby." He pulled the chain to turn on the bedside light. Lisa was on her knees with the sheets held in her lap. He put the bat down in its usual place behind the door and gave her a hard look.

Lisa thought quickly. "Well, why the devil did you have that bat?" she said. Maybe she caught Paul off guard, but maybe not.

"It had fallen on the floor is all," he replied with too much condescension. "I was putting it back. But admit it. You were scared I was Terrance. Admit you think he's capable of sneaking in here and hurting you."

"No! I mean, I don't know. It was only because you were out of the house." She didn't want to lie, but she was so afraid of Paul and Terrance getting into a fight. "Anyway," she added, "he knows I've got your gun right here. He's not so stupid as to want to see that thing again."

"Don't ever bet on stupid," Paul said. He began to undress for bed.

"You're sure you're okay, baby?"

"It's been a long day. I just need some sleep."

20

Always. Be. Closing.

It was not the kind of energy to be carrying into an important meeting, but Lisa had little choice. As she rode the elevator up to her floor, she smoothed her skirt and fluffed her hair and tried to get Paul and Terrance out of her mind.

The truth was Lisa had been far more nervous than she let on. She knew she'd left Jazmin with the burden of the last few days of prep, and she expressed her gratitude repeatedly, but she still felt not only guilty but just out of step, off her game. She tried to quiet the little voice inside that worried about any kind of nonsense, like that she would somehow flub it, or that they were way off base with their approach, or even that Jazmin would somehow use her family problems against her. The kinds of things that nerves could convince one of.

Perhaps it was the added adrenaline, but the ladies were on fire that day. Their preparation paid off: they spoke confidently, their timing was precise, they played off of each other like seasoned performers. The clients weren't immediately sold, but they were visibly and vocally impressed, and their questions showed they were drawn into the main premise despite minor quibbles about negotiable details. By the end of the meeting they had an agreement in principle.

"Excellent work, ladies," Dean told them afterward. "That was just what we were looking for."

"I hope you'll remember this when you talk to the big guy about the Creative Director position," Lisa said.

Dean faked an incredulous look. "You really don't pull your punches do you, Mrs. Drayton?"

"I just know what I want, Mr. Trucco."

"What am I going to do if you become a CD? You're irreplaceable."

"Darn straight. But if you can find someone even half as good as me, you'll be in good shape, I expect."

Jazmin could hardly believe what she was witnessing, and she said so later. "You've got some kind of moxy, girl!"

"Dean's all right, or I wouldn't be quite so brazen. It makes him feel hip, though, to have a black lady talk to him like that."

"Always playing your audience," Jazmin said.

"Always. Be. Closing. Didn't you see that movie—*Glen Garry Glen*, or whatever it was?"

"When do you have time for movies?"

"A girl can't work *all* the time. Come on, let's go get some drinks to celebrate."

21

Dinner Party

Lisa brought Jazmin home that night to join them for a little friendly dinner they'd been planning with Mila and Veronica to meet Mila's new man, Steve. The ladies entered a little tipsy, already, and called for Paul to bring them some wine.

"Congrats, ladies!" said Paul, pouring liberal glasses of pinot grigio. He'd rushed home right after work to put the finishing touches on the dinner prep, which they'd spent a full week putting together in stolen hours of preparation. When Paul raised a glass to toast them, Lisa hesitated and caught his eyes to give him a concerned look. He shrugged her off and said, "To the corporate climbers!" and they clinked their glasses and drank up.

Soon Mila and Steve arrived with two six-packs of local beer—which Paul teased him about—and a salad, and Veronica was not too far behind with a bottle of wine and a loaf of fresh bread. The alcohol flowed freely and helped Jazmin feel quickly at home among the circle of friends talking about work and movies and the weather and the Bears and complaining about public transit and local government.

Because they were among good friends, the evening was not without its rough moments. Too many of them were thinking about Paul's health to completely enjoy themselves, but Steve and Jazmin weren't inner circle enough to bring it up to the whole group. When Paul got up to help Lisa clear the table, Mila followed them into the kitchen and named the elephant in the room.

"How you doing, Paul?" she started.

"Me? I'm fine, just fine." He was scraping plates and handing them to Lisa, who was rinsing them and packing the dishwasher.

"That's good. I mean, you seem fine. What they got you doing now?"

"Who—work?"

"Don't joke with me, Paul. The doctors. What do they have you doing to take care of yourself?"

Paul laughed and shrugged, "Oh, you know, some meds, some dietary changes, normal stuff for now." He looked to his wife with some confusion. "I guess I assumed Lisa told you all this."

"Yeah, I told her," Lisa said. She closed the dishwasher and washed her hands at the sink.

"All right. Let's get back to the party then," Paul suggested.

But Mila said, "I thought you weren't supposed to drink?"

Lisa leaned against the counter with arms folded, waiting, too, for his reply.

"Ah, so that's it? Technically, yes, but tonight…tonight's special—we're celebrating! I'll be back on the diet tomorrow, don't worry."

"It's not you I'm worried about," Mila said.

"Aw, come on." He gestured an appeal to Lisa, but she cocked her head and raised an eyebrow. "I've been good, really. It's just tonight. It'll be all right." He backed away and returned to the dining room, inviting everyone to move to the living room where there were more comfortable seats.

"Ugh, he's so frustrating!" Lisa said, but there was water gathering in her eyes. Mila put a hand on her arm.

"That's men, honey. Just let's get through the night."

Lisa groaned again. "And you know he's gonna want something later when we get up to the bedroom…"

"Well, he can *want* whatever he wants, but that don't mean he can *get* it."

Lisa chuckled but said, "Yeah, you know we ain't like that, though."

"So start being like that. The loudest message you can send a man is to close your legs to him. You give that man too much—and you're prepared to give him even more—for him to flaunt his own health in front of you like that."

"Yeah, but he gets ugly when he's mad *and* drunk," Lisa said and began to return to the party. Mila wasn't having any of that.

"Wait, what do you mean, 'ugly'? You never said anything about 'ugly.'"

Lisa tried to dodge, but Mila insisted. There was too much going on in their lives for Lisa to play things so casual with her.

"All right, but you have to promise not to freak out." She told Mila about waking up to Paul standing by the bed with a bat. "I don't know what I thought. Part of me thought it was Terrance, but another part of me knew it was him and thought...I don't know, some kind of darkness was finally spilling out of him. But you know how he's always been. It's complicated."

"If he puts a hand on you..."

"He didn't, and he won't. Come on, let's get back."

The others had started sharing childhood stories. Jazmin was telling them about growing up with Persian immigrant parents, which got everyone onto analogous stories of their own parents' contradictory strictness and neglect. This was Lisa's least favorite subject, but she just smiled and kept quiet, looking for an opportunity to change the subject.

Jazmin was saying her parents wouldn't let her so much as look at a boy when she was little—unless they were at a Persian party, in which case all the kids would be sent downstairs while the parents drank a fizzy yogurt drink called *doogh*. But the boys and girls would more or less naturally separate themselves out, anyway. She told how they'd stay way past her bedtime and how she often fell asleep in the corners of rooms or in closets or on beds full of coats.

It turned out most of them had a story about their parents staying late at a party, though Paul and Steve recalled having to be dragged away. Veronica said her parents were usually the hosts, so her problem was wanting everyone else to leave.

Of course, they were much more excited about sharing dating stories. Steve and Paul talked themselves up as players, while Veronica was more self-deprecating, admitting she'd never even dated till after high school.

"It was complicated at our school," Mila said. "There were more black and Latino kids than white kids, but, like, the black girls would get mad at you if you dated a black boy."

"That's right," said Veronica. "You white witches already get everything else. What you need our men for?"

"Well, I didn't say nothing when Lisa was dating that white boy, and there were fewer of them to go around!"

"Wait, so you dated white guys in school?" Jazmin asked.

"Just the one. And he was my only real high school boyfriend," Lisa said. "There were only a couple boys who took any note of me, and they were white boys in the honors and AP classes I was in."

"No!" Veronica jumped in. "There was plenty of black boys eying your fair pigments, they was just too dumb for you."

"Oh, so you were smart, too?" Jazmin said.

"What, does that surprise you?" Lisa teased.

"Lisa was always good at school," Mila added. "She was a real nerd."

"*Really?*" said Jazmin, voicing everyone's excitement at the new topic. "I don't believe it!"

"Oh, yeah. Big nerdy glasses and nice sweaters and blouses and stuff. Sometimes it was just her and this boy—and he was a white boy too—battling it out for top of the class."

"Was that your boyfriend?" Steve asked.

"Robbie? Oh no, he couldn't stand me. Robbie thought he owned that school. No, the boy I dated was only smarter than me at geometry. That was the one class I just could not get my head around."

"I was never good at anything," Jazmin said, "and there were no Persian boys at my school, so I could look but I couldn't touch."

"I only ever dated black men, but I can't say that's been working out so well for me," said Veronica. "Lisa had a bunch of black guys in college. But I guess they didn't work out either—lucky for Paul."

"It wasn't that many guys," Paul corrected.

"But they were fine!" said Veronica, licking her lips.

"They were all either too high-minded or too focused on sports and girls," Lisa said. "I was looking for someone who wanted me for me, not for my ideals or my adoration."

Mila held her glass to her lips as she said, "Well, you deserve to be adored, yourself," and then took a long sip. Veronica huffed in assent. Steve felt the barbs in the words without comprehending them, but Paul took her meaning well enough.

"I dated an Asian girl, once," Steve threw out, casually trying to break the tension. "She was nice too. But I wouldn't say it was anything about her being Asian that led to us breaking up."

"What *would* you say?" asked Jazmin.

"What do you want me to say—that she was a bad driver?"

Some friendly jeering and laughter let him off the hook.

Veronica said, "Mila, you've had the smorgasbord of men, what do you think?"

"Smorgasbord?" Steve said.

"Oh, yeah, she just about dated herself around the world, I'd guess."

"And I haven't found any color or country where men aren't dogs," said Mila.

"What, even me?" Steve said with a mock frown.

"Don't kid yourself," Mila scolded back. "You just haven't used up all my dogs-endurance yet."

Jazmin asked Lisa how she and Paul had met.

"I, uh, used to be a cop," Paul said quickly, "and I'd see her around on the street. One day I asked her out."

"That's sweet," said Jazmin.

"But it's only half the story," said Lisa. "He left out the part where he was harassing me and my friends on the street for no reason and I gave him a piece of my mind."

"Oh," Jazmin said, confused as to just how to react to this.

"Yeah, well, that's not exactly a part of the story I'm proud of," said Paul.

"It's all right. I set your racist butt straight."

"It wasn't about racism," Paul insisted as if he was tired of having to make the point. "It was just what we were supposed to do. Anyway, I'm done with all that. The point is: she impressed me."

"That's sweet," said Jazmin, eager to accentuate the positive. "What impressed you?"

"I'm not even sure *I've* heard this," Mila said, leaning forward.

"All right, all right. Well, obviously she was beautiful, for starters. And she had spirit, which you've all seen plenty of for yourselves, I'm sure. And then she was so smart and well-spoken about her… grievances."

"'Well-spoken,' my, my," said Veronica. "All's I know is I ain't never been accused a that."

As Lisa enjoyed the stories and shared in the friendly laughter, she felt a kind of sadness. She didn't begrudge her friends their memories; she just wished she could have the same kind of distance from her own so she could laugh at them, almost treasure them. Her own memories were like a bad movie she was happy to forget she'd ever seen.

Except no one would ever let her forget them, it seemed. Inevitably, someone asked Lisa to share one of her own stories—it was Jazmin, who could be forgiven for not knowing better, but Mila, Veronica, and Paul had always been of the joint opinion that it would be better for her to talk about her past.

"No, I don't really have a lot of good stories from growing up," she dodged.

"It's all right, there must be *some*thing!"

"Not much that's good, I'm afraid. More wine?"

"Sure, thanks. But tell me about your family. Do you have any siblings?"

Paul scoffed, which was perhaps an appropriate response, but it po'ed Lisa anyway.

"Just a brother," she acknowledged, "but we're not on good terms."

"*That's* an understatement," Paul added. "That fool attacked her the other day."

"Attacked?" said Steve, who did not know what minefield he was entering.

"He needed money. Again," said Paul. "And he seems to think his sister is his own personal bank. When she stood up to him this time, he got ugly about it."

All eyes were on Lisa, who could have smacked her husband for airing her family's dirty laundry in front of her co-worker. Mila took the opportunity to punch Paul in the arm and whisper, "You're drunk. Shut the freek up," in his ear.

"Yes, it was ugly," Lisa said, "and thank God it's over. But I don't want to talk about it right now."

"Oh, I'm sorry," Jazmin said.

"It's not your fault, Jazmin," Paul said, ignoring Mila. "Lisa likes to pretend like she doesn't have a family most days. She has some kind of complex about coming from the hood. Anybody says anything and she gets mad at them."

Lisa was fuming, as was Mila. "I never said I was mad," she tried to say calmly. "I just don't want to talk about it. It's over now."

"Yeah, don't worry, I saw to that."

"What does that mean?"

"It means I had a little talk with Terrance."

"I thought I told you *not* to?"

"It seemed like the right call, anyway. I think he got the message."

"I think we should talk about this later," Lisa said slowly, trying to stay in control.

"Oh, boy," Paul said. "That's her code for, 'Later, I'm going to tell you what I think, and you're going to sit there and take it if you ever want any loving again.'"

The women flinched and avoided eye contact with one another. Steve chuckled good-naturedly but Mila's elbow in his ribs told him he had misread the situation.

When they had seen their guests to the door and said their goodbyes, Lisa turned and walked wordlessly back to the kitchen to tidy up. Paul crept up behind her at the counter and tried to put his arms around her.

He began to say, "Hey, this stuff can wait—" but she squirmed away from him without so much as looking at him.

"Aw, come on," Paul whined. "Let's keep celebrating."

"You can celebrate on your own…if you can 'celebrate' at all in your condition."

"What's this about?"

"I'm not sure I want to talk about it right now."

"Then when are we gonna talk about it?"

"All right: you were an idiot tonight. You happy now?"

"What did *I* do?"

"You got blind drunk and embarrassed me with that talk about my family and you po'd me off going to talk to T behind my back. That sound like enough?"

"All right, I shouldn't have talked to your brother. I don't know what makes you think I could *not* talk to him, but okay."

"You could have gotten hurt—or hurt him. And anyway, I told you to leave it."

"I'm sorry, baby," Paul said. He got his arm around her and tried to kiss her cheek, but she pulled away; she hated when his apologies came wrapped around a desire for sex.

"Paul, no, not now."

"Oh, come on. Water under the bridge."

"Not yet, it isn't. Let's just go to bed."

"You been avoiding me."

"No, I haven't."

"You have. You're haven't embarrassed me 'cause I'm sick. That's why I went after Terrance—to show you I can still protect you."

"Oh, yeah, you a real big man, struttin' your stuff like that," Lisa snarled. "That's what's pathetic, not your kidney disease." She threw the washcloth on the sink and left the kitchen, abandoning the dishes.

"Pathetic?" Paul called after her. "Pathetic? Yeah, you walk away and tell me who's pathetic. I've had about enough of your lack of respect, you know that?"

But she was already upstairs and would not give him the satisfaction of a response.

22

A Shot in the Dark

A woman lay in a bed in the blue dark night. A man stood over her. The bedsheet had slid off her as she turned in the bed. The moonlight curved silver-blue over her body, and he could see the slow inhalation and exhalation of breath, though he could only hear his own heavy puffing.

It was not the sleep one might expect of a woman with something on her mind. The man's fist tightened around a baseball bat as if her very peacefulness offended him. He slowly raised it, like a man who had imagined such a moment in his mind but could not quite figure out the motions.

Outside, a door slammed, and at the same instant the man brought the bat down on the woman's arm.

The woman awoke screaming and curled up into a ball then tried to roll around the bed to avoid the blows.

"No! No, stop!" she shrieked, but still the blows fell. "Why are you doing this! Please!"

"Shut up! Shut up!" the man shrieked back.

She knew the man, you could see it in her eyes, which is why she didn't roll off the bed altogether and hide in the corner. She believed he would stop if she screamed enough.

He did not stop. He swung at her arms, her legs, her buttocks, her stomach. Some swings missed altogether. It was sloppy. A tantrum more than an attack. He swung to make a point, but not to kill. Not exactly.

149

"No! Please! Stop!"

"Shut! Up!"

As she shrunk up in the top corner of the bed, he began to come around, but then she lunged for the bedside table. He beat her there and pulled out the pistol.

"Don't even think about it, you witch!" he said, and threw the gun into the hallway. Then he jabbed her in the breast with the end of the bat.

Her screams became more desperate. She hardly spoke words so much as whined desperate noises.

"Stop, please, stop!"

And then he did stop, froze in place as if sucker-punched in the kidney. They were both vaguely aware that there had been a percussive shock. They sought some clue to the mystery in each other's eyes, but there was none. Then suddenly the man dropped the bat and collapsed onto the floor.

The phone rang next to the bed. Lisa rolled over and peeked at the caller ID.

"What the devil?" she muttered and hit the reject button.

Paul mumbled a question, and she answered him that it was nothing.

The phone rang again, and again Lisa looked at the caller ID and rejected it.

The phone rang a third time. Paul suggested it was probably the wrong number and she should answer and tell them.

"It's my mother," she admitted.

"Maybe it's important," he said.

"I don't want to talk to her."

Paul lifted himself with a great sigh and reached over to grab the receiver.

"Joyce, what do you want?" he said into it. "What...? *What?*"

Something in his tone got Lisa's attention. Her heart began to race despite herself. She didn't want to care, but she was trying to make out what her mother was saying.

"Where is he now?… What about Yolanda and the kids?… All right, all right, we're coming."

Paul hung up the phone and looked Lisa dead in the eyes.

"Your brother's been shot."

Lisa pushed him away and sat up. "What? When? Where is he?" There were fireworks in her head. *Terrance? Shot?* In all the drama of the past few days, all the drama of her life, her brother's life, she'd somehow never really believed this could happen. Some part of her brain was explaining it away as a mistake, as an impossibility. It was like she'd just fallen overboard without a life vest, the cold waters drawing her down to their unforgiving depths.

"I don't know," Paul told her. "Maybe a couple hours ago. He's at Providence. Your mother…"

"My mother *what?*"

"She needs a ride."

If she'd felt like she was drowning before, now she felt like someone had tied a weight to her feet. It was an old, old, too-familiar feeling. Her mother never lifted you up; she just tried to take you down with her.

"No," Lisa said.

"What?" For all he knew about their relationship, she surprised Paul with this. In fact, she surprised herself.

"Call her a cab."

Lisa rose and started to dress, so Paul did the same.

"Are you crazy?" he said.

"Any other time she'd figure it out herself. If she was in a hurry to get there she'd get a neighbor or call her own cab, but instead she calls us. A time like this and she's playing her little games already!"

"Well, we can't just leave her there," Paul said as they left the bedroom. Lisa didn't fight back, which was as close to a concession as he was going to get.

Lisa stayed in the car when they arrived at Joyce's house. The two women didn't even greet one another when Joyce took her seat in the back.

When Paul couldn't stand the tense silence any longer, he said, "How did you find out, Joyce?"

"Yolander call me from the hospital" was all she said.

"Do we know who did it?"

"Yolander say *she* do, but she in shock. She don't know what she saying."

Paul decided not to press the question.

"Things were always so tough for that boy," Joyce suddenly said. They could hear she was actually crying. "Nothing ever turned out right for him. Nobody ever gave him no breaks."

Lisa's whole body tensed up, preparing for an attack. Paul reached over and gently squeezed her knee. She put a grateful hand on top of his and breathed deeply.

"I did what I could for him, you know," Joyce carried on. "He and I, we only have each other. Yolander don't support him like she oughtta…"

They hoped by not responding she would eventually lose steam, but she hadn't said what she'd wanted to yet.

"I shore wish you coulda spared him a few dollas," she added. Her voice was rueful, as if lamenting something inevitable and long in the past. "Just a few, to tide him over. What's it to you? You got those fancy jobs. You ain't got no kids. Just a few dollas is all."

Paul squeezed her hand again to tell her to hang on. She was breathing forcefully through her nose now. Big, dragon breaths. Another couple minutes and they'd be at the hospital.

"This maybe all coulda been avoided, seems to me," said Joyce as if thinking out loud.

"Momma, this is *not* my fault!" Lisa said at last. "We still don't know what even happened."

"Baby, I'm not trying to say whose fault it is," Joyce said. "I'm just saying if some folks had just helped Terrance out he might not have gotten into any trouble like this. I don't see how a few bucks woulda been so hard for you two, that's all."

"Momma, it's never just a few bucks. It's a hundred here, three hundred there."

"How much this car cost?" Joyce asked.

"Joyce, please," Paul said. "This isn't about the money. I gave T a couple hundred the other day, okay, and this still happened, so can we please leave it be."

Lisa couldn't believe what she was hearing, but she didn't want to fight with Paul in front of her mother. The confession shut her up for the time being, anyway.

Terrance woke up with a sensation like rats clawing through his side. The house was dark, and he heard a crowd of people quickly running down the stairs. He still wasn't sure what had happened, but something in his brain said, "*Run!*"

He'd learned to trust that voice. He believed it was why he'd survived as long as he had. Only moments before, it had told him to drop the bat, and for the first time he had ignored it, and look where it got him.

He wasn't sure if he could stand. Just getting up onto his hands and knees winded him. He realized he was in a pool of his own blood, which made his head reel. Breathing carefully, he crawled to the stairs and sat up at the top one. He used the rail to brace himself as he slid down one stair at a time, but with each landing he felt like something was going fall out of him.

It seemed like there was blood everywhere, so much blood. He tried to imagine it all having once flowed through his veins. He tried to believe there was enough left to get him out of there.

The back door was hanging open. Yolanda and the kids must have left that way. He swung it wide and pushed himself through the storm door. As soon as he was outside, Rosita bounded up and began to lick his face and hands. For a moment, he simply accepted her affections; it felt good to have someone's love, still. But when she started sniffing around his wound and licking the blood, he pushed her away and started scooting down the back stairs.

At the bottom he stopped again, catching his breath. The lights were on in the house next door, and Mrs. Johnson was standing in her kitchen window just watching him. He wanted to yell something tough, but he couldn't make his mouth work. She'd known him since he was a boy; it was embarrassing to think she was looking at him now shaking her head and thinking he had turned out to be just another dead street punk.

Across the alley someone was playing music. Sam Cooke sang, *"It's been too hard living/but I'm afraid to die."*

Terrance heard the words and tried not to laugh at the joke. He crawled a few feet then a few more. Down the alley he thought he heard Yolanda's voice, and one of the boys. There may have been another voice, a man, but he couldn't hear what anyone was saying.

Then he saw blue and red flashers reflecting off the bushes and the garage. That had probably been Mrs. Johnson, and whatever she was thinking would be more or less right, after all. With a grunt, he fell into the grass and lay there looking at the sky, looking for the stars past the pale orange glow of the eternal city lights. *"It's been a lo-ong time coming/But a change is gonna come."*

When Paul, Lisa, and Joyce arrived at the hospital, Terrance was still in surgery. They were led to another room where Yolanda was in a bed, an IV hooked up to her right hand and her gown hanging off her left shoulder, revealing a bandage across her left breast. Tommy was sitting in a chair by the window playing with Tammy in his lap.

"It went right through T, they said," Yolanda told them, "and caught me right in the breast. I lost a bit of blood getting over here, but other than that they said it slowed down a lot going through Terrance and hit the fleshy part of my breast, so I'm pretty lucky."

"Honey, I'm so sorry," Lisa said, sitting down beside her on the bed. "Where's Michael?"

"He with my dad. He was gone take all the kids back, but I said I wanted Tammy with me, and Tommy stayed to help with the baby."

"Well, can you tell us what happened?"

"That's no kind of talk right now," Joyce said. She had more or less ignored Yolanda and gone to be with her grandkids. Yolanda did indicate the children with her eyes, so Paul offered to take them to the cafeteria for something to eat. Paul tried to get Joyce to come, too, offering to buy her some pie.

"Why don't we all go?" she said. "Give Yolander some time to rest."

"We just got here," said Lisa. "I'd like to stay a bit, if it's okay with Yolanda." Yolanda said she wouldn't mind the company, and Joyce stayed, too, though she grumped about it as though she'd been forced.

"So tell me then," Lisa said.

"Somebody broke into the house!" Joyce cried. "There was somebody else there! It had to been."

Her mother's report scared Lisa, but also confused her.

"Joyce, please, she deserves to know," Yolanda said.

"You don't know what you're saying," Joyce insisted. "You shouldn't go talking like that."

"It's too late, Joyce," said Yolanda. "I already told the police everything. It's on the record now."

"What is?" Lisa said. "What the devil happened?"

"You a crazy Delilah, you is," Joyce grumbled and sat with a huff.

Yolanda told Lisa how Terrance had attacked her. She mentioned the bat, but she downplayed the severity of the beating itself, acting like he only hit her a couple times, as if that would make it sound better.

"He'd already gone after me—and the kids, the psycho—a few days ago. The boys got real scared and mad. It's been real bad around the house lately..." she broke off to sob for a minute then continued. "I be honest with you, I was scared and mad too. I been thinking for a long time now I don't know how much I can take of this man's craziness. So when he was waving that bat, something in me sorta snapped, you know? I went for the gun in the side table..."

"Oh, honey," Lisa said. She knew from recent experience all too well how scary Terrance could be. And she wasn't surprised to hear Terrance beat Yolanda sometimes. Taking a bat to her, however, was another level. It meant he was losing it. And then to have his own wife go for a gun. Two of the most important women in his life pull a gun on him within days of each other?

"I wasn't going to do nothing but get his attention," Yolanda was saying. "I don't even know how to use it, for goodness sake. He threw it away, into the hallway. It was only a moment or so more before I heard it go off. He just froze, standing over me, holding the bat up and with this funny look on his face like I just growed two heads or something. Then his arm starts slowly falling, like, and then he drops the bat, and we still both trying to figure out what was going on. I didn't even feel the bullet hit me cause of the adrenaline and all, but I start to see blood spreading on his shirt. Then he fell down…just like a puppet or something…"

Lisa had to hold her hand over her mouth to keep herself from crying out. It was all too gruesome.

"And then," Yolanda continued, "and then…I saw Michael… and he was…he was holding…the gun…"

Lisa felt like she was being suffocated. She made a gagging noise and held onto the railing of the bed. Yolanda was a mess of tears. Joyce cried from her corner, "No! No! It's not true! You lying! You seeing things! You stop talking like this!"

A nurse heard the commotion and peeked her head in. Lisa had the presence of mind to nod over at her mother. The nurse went over to Joyce and crouched down beside her. "Ma'am, this has been a tough night for you all. Let me take you to get some coffee or tea or something."

"She's *lying*!" Joyce kept yelling, but she didn't resist when the nurse gently helped her stand and led her out of the room.

Lisa couldn't process what she had just heard. She wanted to know how it was possible. She wanted to know exactly what happened. She wanted to insist, as her mother had, that it was impossible, that it must have been otherwise, but she couldn't ask anything of the woman who lay beside her with such a hollowed out look to her. And what answers could suffice for the depths of the questions?

But their tears, shed over this family horror, began to do a work in Lisa that no amount of criticism and judgment and accusation had been able to do. The night's violence pierced her defenses, and for the first time in possibly decades she saw Yolanda not as a feature of her broken past but as a sister, a common traveler through this vale of tears.

23

Investigation

Terrance was in the operating room another hour or so. No one knew or much cared. Time had taken on the shape of a foreign custom that they could only hear about as about something other people did. Paul brought the kids back, in better moods for having had some food. Joyce had returned, too, and sat petting the baby and grumbling to herself, pouting in general that Yolanda had blabbed her crazy theory to Lisa, who at some point pulled Paul into the hall and told him. A doctor came in to report that Terrance was in the recovery room and they'd come get them when he woke up. Joyce insisted she go down right away, so the doctor beckoned a nurse to take her.

They put on the TV to distract the kids, though the inane cartoon they were watching was a welcome anchor to the world of ordinary people and things.

The sun began to light the parking lot outside the window, and they'd just started their third or fourth cartoon, when a man in a gray sports jacket and striped tie, slightly loosened, came into the room and introduced himself to Paul and Lisa as Detective Kaminsky. He asked Yolanda if he could ask her a few follow-up questions. She assented and said she preferred the family stayed.

"Very well," said Kaminsky. "So Forensics has finished going through the house, and I want to double check a few details so we can get a clear picture of what happened. Could you just describe again for me what happened?"

"I'm sorry, is this really necessary?" Lisa interrupted. "How many times is she going to have to relive this today?"

"I'm sorry, ma'am, but it really is the best way to get to the truth," Kaminski said.

"She's told you the truth!" Lisa replied, but Paul his hand on her knee and gave her an assuring look.

"I don't doubt it, ma'am," said Kaminsky, "but sometimes when we go back through the event, new details emerge. Now, Mrs. McNight...?"

Yolanda recounted the evening much as she had for Lisa, if with less emotion. Lisa flinched to hear her making excuses for Terrance's violence, but she held her peace. Detective Kaminsky was particularly interested in the events immediately after the shooting, between the time Terrance collapsed and when the police arrived. Yolanda said that was fuzzier because she was in such a panic, but explained how she was horrified to see her son holding the gun, how she needed to get her kids out of there, how they ran to her father's house two blocks away, and he had taken them to the hospital when he saw she'd been injured.

"Did you direct your father not to speak with the police, Mrs. McNight?"

"No, why? He not talking to you?"

"No, ma'am."

Yolanda began to cry. "He must be worried you gone take Michael from us. But you're not, is you?"

"Ma'am, I had the same idea, and I assure you we're not planning to take Michael away. To be honest, it looks like a straightforward case of domestic violence getting ugly because there was a firearm in the house. Your son was trying to protect his mama, so we'd chalk it up to self-defense. We'd still like to talk to Michael, though, but we don't want to scare your father away. If you could let him know it's okay to talk to us, it'd be a real help. It's Terrance that should be worried."

Det. Kaminsky asked if it was okay to ask Tommy some questions, and both he and Yolanda said it was. Tommy didn't have much to tell, and he'd told it to the detective once already that morning. He and Michael woke up when they heard their mother screaming. They listened at the door for a while before venturing into the hallway and looking in. Tommy heard Tammy screaming in her crib, so he bade Michael come with him to get the baby.

He went to Tammy's room, picked her up, and rocked her in his arms for a minute. Then he heard the bang, which he recognized as a gun. He cried in a loud whisper for Michael to hide, and he ducked into the corner behind the crib. It was not long after that that he realized Michael wasn't in the room, but he couldn't say when he'd left. When he went to see what had happened, he saw Michael standing in the hallway with the gun in his hand.

Each time Lisa heard the story she tried to believe it would somehow turn out differently, but it did not. Her brother had attacked his wife with a bat, and his own son had shot him. This had happened. Her family had become a tawdry ghetto story you hear on the evening news.

She tried to imagine returning to her nice house with her nice lawn and her nice hedges. A golden gate closed over that whole life and left her shaking the bars, trying in vain to justify herself to the respectable world on the other side. The doctors. Her colleagues. Her husband. *It's not me. This is not me.*

24

Between

So many questions, they all kept thinking, but it was really only the one question, the weight of which amplified it and multiplied it in their minds: *Why?* Why did this happen? Why did Terrance attack his wife? Why couldn't he get his life together? Why didn't they do this or say that when they had the chance? Why didn't anybody do any of the thousands of little graces and mercies that maybe, just maybe, could have added up to salvation for poor Terrance McNight?

Poor Terrance, everyone kept saying. *Poor Terrance.* It befuddled and irritated the hospital staff. They only saw the drug-addled OR case who had attacked his wife and been shot by his own child in an act of poetic justice. They didn't see, because they couldn't possibly see, the countless tiny moments in the young man's life that molded and built and chipped away at his personality until he was the strung-out, broke, and broken shell of a person currently being sewn up on the operating table.

A new doctor came in and introduced herself as the surgeon who had operated on Terrance. Joyce scowled, probably unconsciously, not sure if this woman surgeon was up to the task of saving her boy. Even Lisa had to fight a surprise impulse to suspect her, but she was quickly distracted by the news they were hearing.

"The good news is we've stabilized him," the doctor was saying. "He had some severe internal bleeding, and his internal organs are not in great shape. We stopped the bleeding and stitched up what we could. The bullet entered his back on the right side and exited through his abdomen. I'm afraid it completely destroyed his kidney, and we had to remove it."

They gasped and murmured and looked to the doctor for help understanding.

"We don't have all our tests back yet, but my guess, just from his vitals and the condition of the kidney we removed is that the other one is not performing adequately. I think we need to prepare ourselves for the very strong possibility that he will need a donor kidney in the very near future."

Lisa, who had been standing, suddenly sat down. Paul's face went gray and he became even more sober.

"A donor kidney?" Joyce said. "My boy? Take mine! What do I need to do?"

"Of course, ma'am," said the doctor. "I'm happy to know you feel that way. The waiting list will probably not be an option in this case. I recommend you all get tested to see if you're a match, and we can take things from there."

The surgeon left the room, and they all sat in the silent depths of their own reflections, unable to even look at one another.

At length Yolanda croaked, "Thank you, Joyce."

They all traded surprised looks; few people ever said that to the woman. She rarely did anything to earn real gratitude.

"He's my baby," she said. "Anything. Anything."

"I'll get tested too," Yolanda said. "Just in case."

"Well, if I can't do it, prob'ly Lisa can," Joyce stated. "We'll take care of him."

Lisa and Paul did not respond with the eagerness or affirmation Joyce expected. Instead, Lisa started to cry.

"Mama, you have to know something," Lisa sobbed, but Paul interrupted her.

"No, baby, it's okay. Forget about it. He's your brother."

"Forget about what?" said Joyce.

"Mama, Paul's sick."

"Yeah? Sick with what?"

"It's a disease…in his kidneys."

Joyce grew stern and seemed to coil up—either to attack or to escape.

"I've already been tested and approved to donate a kidney to *him*," Lisa concluded.

Yolanda stifled a cry, but Joyce rose and started toward her daughter.

"Joyce, hold on," Paul said, standing between them. "Don't listen to her. If you can't be a donor, I'll understand. I'm not going to come between her and her brother."

"Well, that's sensible of you," Joyce scoffed.

"Paul, Mama, it's not your choice," Lisa said.

"That's right," said Joyce. "It's yours, and you got to stick with your family."

"I don't 'got' to do anything, Mama. I made my choice."

"Why, you little pale-skinned master syndrome-loving witch," Joyce seethed.

"Joyce, Lisa, please," Paul tried.

"You gone turn your back on your fambly? You gone let your brother die? Blood is thicker than water, isn't it?"

"Joyce, we don't even know that you can't be the donor. Let's just calm down for a minute and take things one step at a time."

"It's like I don't even have a daughter. I may as well not, for all the good she does us."

"I don't need to sit here taking this abuse," Lisa said. The quaver in her voice and the tears forming in her eyes betrayed her hurt and anger, but she strutted out of the room like a person taking the higher ground, saying only, "I'm sorry, Yolanda, I really am," as she closed the door behind her.

Paul threw Joyce a nasty look and followed his wife. They walked down long halls and took an elevator to the main lobby and then stepped outside into the midmorning sun that was already hinting at the heat of afternoon.

"Where are we going?" Paul finally asked.

"I don't know. Ennis's ain't even open yet."

"I don't know if a drink is a good idea right now."

"I didn't say it was a good idea. It's just better than staying in a room with that woman any longer."

"Can't argue with that."

"If I smoked I suppose I'd have a cigarette or four about now."

"Come here." Paul embraced her. She resisted at first, holding her anger, but she never could withstand his affection for long. She let herself soften into his chest, and then all the emotion came out in sloppy heaves and gasps.

"Did you mean what you said back there?" she asked when she had caught her breath.

"I think I did," he answered. "But I appreciate your commitment."

"Paul," she said, keeping her face pressed against his chest so she didn't meet his eyes, "if I'm being totally honest, all that bluster in there was mostly about my mother pushing me around. When the doctor said Terrance might need a kidney, my first thought was that I should give him one of mine."

Paul let this sink in. "Oh," he said.

"Not instead of you," Lisa tried to explain. "For just a moment I wanted to give you each one, like it wasn't impossible, you know?"

Paul wanted to understand, he really did, but it wasn't as simple as that.

"Paul, he's my brother. What am I supposed to do?"

She fell apart in more tears while her strong but sick husband held her and had no words to say.

When they returned to Yolanda's room they were told Terrance was awake and in another room to recover. Joyce had already gone to see him with the kids, and Lisa wanted to see him, too, so they left Yolanda alone again.

They found Terrance lying in a bed with several tubes connected to him, watching his mother. Detective Kaminsky and an officer were in the room, and Joyce was frantically talking at them. She had suddenly become convinced that the way to protect Terrance was to give the police Michael. She was explaining how Yolanda had spoiled the child and turned him against his father and how they needed to rein in this infant monster and teach him a lesson to set him straight.

"Mama, please," Lisa broke in. "Excuse me, Detective. Officer, I'm Terrance's sister, Lisa."

"Officer Keys. I'm assisting Det. Kaminsky in his investigation. Your mother has just been telling us about her grandson."

"I gathered. I love my brother, but I hope you don't think a six-year-old boy is capable of deliberately hurting his own father."

"We're just gathering perspectives and information, ma'am," said Det. Kaminsky. "However, we were just explaining to Mrs. McNight here that we will be taking your brother into custody as soon as he's released from the hospital."

Joyce grumbled some uncomplimentary things, but Lisa said, "Is that really necessary?"

"Yes, ma'am. I believe you've seen your sister-in-law's arms. There are more bruises on her shoulders, back, hips, and thighs. That's more than enough to constitute domestic battery. And then there's illegal possession of a firearm and possession of narcotics. Unless those were Yolanda's…"

"Oh my god," Lisa gasped. Paul guided her to a chair.

"What narcotics are we talking about here, Detective?" Paul asked.

"Just cannabis."

"*Just?*" Lisa asked.

"No jail time, just a fee," Paul explained. "Still, he's looking at up to two years and some fines he won't be able to pay."

"Y'all don't understand what this boy lives with," Joyce shouted, turning on the police. "He works his butt off for his family, and they don't give two cents about him."

"Are you prepared now to tell us the nature of this 'work,' ma'am?" Kaminsky said, raising his eyebrows.

Joyce was instantly confused and even looked hurt, like she'd been tricked. "I told you he always changing jobs and doing odd things. I don't know all what he do."

Terrance coughed hoarsely and seemed about to say something, but then he looked away and closed his eyes. Joyce couldn't handle it anymore and ran from the room in desperate tears. Det. Kaminsky said they were through but that they'd have to keep an officer at the door until Terrance was released, and Officer Keys was taking first shift. Paul offered to check on Joyce, and now Lisa was alone with her brother for the first time since he'd come over just days before.

She stood beside his bed and, without even noticing she did it, picked up his limp hand.

"Terrance," she whispered. "You *fool*. What have you done?"

Terrance surprised her by opening his eyes. He gave her his wry, you're-not-mad-at-*me*-are-you smile. She looked away to hide her own smile in return.

"Here I thought...it was...you...who'd blow me a—...way."

His voice was breathy and his humor forced.

"You idiot," Lisa said, trying to sound scornful. "Maybe if I had, poor little Michael..."

"Would you...really...have done it?" he asked her.

"Were you really gonna do something to me?" she asked right back.

Terrance looked like he was thinking as carefully about the question as she was, following the trail of mixed-up emotions that led to that dark path on which all manner of horrors became suddenly plausible.

She kissed him on the head and put her other hand on his shoulder.

"Best not to dwell on that, I think."

The quiet between them was an intimacy, a space for the memories of past affection, if not a space entirely of peace.

"I'm glad...you're...here," Terrance said.

"How could I not be?" Lisa mused.

"The way...we treat you...I wouldn't...blame you...But I always...knew...you'd stick by...me."

"I guess that's what families do."

"If Mama...give me her...kidney,...she'll really...have...her claws in me."

"Yeah she will, T. She'll own your butt more'n she do now."

"I might just...opt to die then," he wheezed. He was smiling, but Lisa couldn't smile with him, not about this.

"Try to get her...off the...Michael thing," he said. "It wasn't... his fault."

"She's the only one in the world who would possibly think it was."

"I really...did it this...time."

"Yes, you did." The tears returned to her eyes.

"Whatever hap-pens, don't...leave me."

She didn't respond, only held his hand and stood beside him as the silence wrapped them up again and he drifted off to sleep.

25

Waiting

The next forty-eight hours could have been forty-eight days. It wasn't so much that a lot happened as that there were long spells of inactivity and waiting between short periods of receiving news and updates. Terrance's wounds stabilized, but his surviving kidney was not performing as they'd hoped. No one had heard from Yolanda's father and thus no one was quite sure where Tommy and Michael were. Yolanda was released around noon the first day since her injury was rather minor, and she went home to make calls and try to find her children. The initial blood tests indicated that Joyce was a potential donor, but they needed to run two more tests to confirm. Lisa was a universal donor, but they would still need to run the same two extra tests.

Lisa's memory of that time was a flurry of pink, green, blue, and floral hospital scrubs. Of sitting in stiff chairs until she had to get up and move then pacing until she didn't see the point in that, either, and sitting back down. Of staring at the gray and black roofs of restaurants and department stores from their tenth floor window and wondering how the tiny people in their toy cars could possibly be carrying on with their lives when a boy had shot his father and two men were doomed to die.

Mila and Veronica came by and stayed for about an hour, alternately comforting her and distracting her with idle talk. Lisa and Paul took several long walks in the neighborhood behind the hospital, stealing a few moments to feel like normal people with normal lives.

"With all the craziness in our lives, all this waiting is almost peaceful," Paul suggested.

"Almost," Lisa shrugged. "If I can forget everything for a second or two."

When they rounded the corner Joyce was standing outside the hospital door. She started waving and shouting. The tests had come back. The doctor wanted Lisa and Joyce both there to discuss them.

"I know we've been over this before," the doctor began, "but I want to remind you that each donor candidate must pass all three screenings in order to be considered a match. Joyce and Lisa, you each passed the first two, the blood type and the tissue-typing. Unfortunately, Joyce, and I know this is hard to hear, but we ran into a problem at the antigen testing phase. The test suggests that Terrance's body would reject your kidney."

"*Reject* it? My own baby's body would reject a piece of *my* body? He my baby!" Joyce started reaching out in the air as if to grab the doctor's words and erase them from the world.

"It is relatively rare, Mrs. McNight, but it does happen. Please try to understand that, if it was going to be this way, it's better to know before we do the surgery than to find out too late. But..."

"But what?"

"Well, Lisa's blood passed the antigen test, meaning she's an eligible donor for her brother."

"O, thank god! Thank god thank god thank god!" Joyce shouted. "My baby gonna be okay. He gonna be okay."

Lisa was staring at a printout the doctor had handed her, not really gleaning anything from it but feeling like she should consult it. She did not see the doctor, who understood the predicament she now found herself in, look upon her with compassionate eyes.

"I have some other patients to check in on," he said. "I'll come find you a little later and we can talk about next steps."

So the worst-case scenario was the actual case. There was no avoiding it, no more waiting and seeing, no more assurances that it would be all right. There was only one way it was going to be all right, and even that wouldn't make it all right. Not at all.

When Lisa returned to Terrance's room, she found her mother there already, in tears of joy, explaining how Lisa was going to help him, how he was going to be okay, how this nightmare was almost over.

Joyce jumped up from her chair, ran to her daughter, and grabbed her hand to drag her over to the bedside. It was a simple, even childlike gesture. Familiar. Lisa stared at their hands, her mother's that pale caramel brown, her own appearing pale beside it, like too much cream in coffee. She couldn't remember the last time her mother touched her. Not even the last time she was slapped across the face or over the head. Now her mother held her hand eagerly, cheerfully, and her brother gave her that happy, slightly abashed grin of his.

She flashed back to when she was seven or eight and she and Terrance had crept into their mother's bed one morning. Who knew the reason? They needed little more reason than the impulse to do it. For a few minutes that morning, their mother lay in bed caressing them, petting their heads, like they were a regular, loving family.

How did that moment end? Probably like most of them did. She and her brother would begin to bicker, her mother would tell them to knock it off, Lisa might take a swipe at Terrance, their mother would slap her back and tell her to get her ugly butt off the bed and leave her brother alone. If that was as bad as it got it would have been a pretty calm morning, but chances are there was yelling and more slapping and even thrown shoes and toys and dishes.

"Mama, we gotta talk," Lisa said, and she hated herself for breaking up the family harmony once again. "I don't know yet what I'm gonna do."

"What do you mean you don't know what you gone do?" Joyce cried. "What choice is there? Your brother or your man? Ain't no man worth coming between you and you own blood. What you talking about, 'don't know what you gone do'?"

"I'm sorry, Mama. I'm sorry, T. I just can't say for sure right now. I don't know how to decide."

169

"I tell you how to decide—" Joyce began, but Terrance interrupted.

"Mama, Mama, don't." He grimaced at his mother and cocked his head toward his sister in a gesture that clearly meant, *What more do you expect from her?*

"Now what the heck is that supposed to mean?" Lisa challenged.

"It's cool, sis," Terrance said. "Ain't no point arguing with you. You was never wrong in your whole damn life, so I suppose you won't be wrong to let your brother die while you spare the life of a white cop just 'cause you sleeping with him."

Lisa slapped him hard across the face and called him some choice things she wasn't accustomed to calling people. Joyce screamed and wrapped Lisa up in a bear hug to pull her away from the bed.

"Let me go, Mama," Lisa said, and Joyce let her go but immediately started in on hitting her.

"You ungrateful, stupid, ugly witch!" her mother was saying as she pounded on her daughter's arms and back. "You never loved us! You never loved us!"

"*I* never loved *you*?" Lisa replied, backing away but not backing down. "This what you call love, beating on your children?"

"How I'm supposed to love a stupid, ugly, selfish witch like you?" Joyce screamed, still attacking.

At last a nurse appeared and separated the women, threatening to call the police, which got Joyce to at least lower her volume and sit down while she insulted her daughter. The nurse spoke with authority but also respect and kindness, and Joyce began to simmer down.

Where was this nurse all my life? Lisa thought to herself. *Can I hire her to keep Mama outta my face all the time?*

But she couldn't joke with herself for long. It didn't feel like she could do anything for long.

26

Pressed

After the nurse left, they sat in a tense silence. Lisa didn't dare speak lest she set her mother off on some complaint or another. Terrance breathed heavily and looked ready to fall asleep again. Joyce mumbled to herself on and off until she finally announced she needed a smoke and fled the room.

Her mother took a dark, heavy cloud with her, and Lisa felt like she could breathe again. The sun warmed the room and the machines made a pleasant low hum, and she slumped in her chair and even thought she could take a nap.

But her mind would not leave her alone. She blamed Terrance. She blamed her mother. She blamed herself. None of it seemed to help.

Terrance fell asleep, so she felt comfortable getting up and taking a walk around the halls. There was something comforting about seeing nurses popping in and out of other rooms. There by the bed it was easy to feel like her life and her family were a disaster, like they among all people could not hold their lives together, but the fact that other people were in those rooms reminded her that hard times fall on everyone, that, as the preacher used to read from the Bible, the rain falls on the righteous and the wicked alike. Only, which one was she?

She found herself in the large atrium at the front of the hospital. It featured a large waterfall streaming down a red marble wall into a shallow pool decorated with mosaic tiles. A mechanical grand piano ground out a solo arrangement of "Let it Be." There were large planters with ferns and ficus trees everywhere, and a few pots of red, pink, and white carnations.

It's like the lobby of a hotel, she thought. It makes you feel like you're traveling, like you're on a little vacation. Is that a good thing or a bad thing? Does it make me more comfortable or is it just an illusion? Do I want to feel more or less like this is real life, like this is where life happens and not in the office or the bar or the bedroom?

But then she noticed a crowd outside a little ways away from the sliding front doors. Some in the crowd had cameras, and some held furry gray and blue boom mics over their heads, pointed toward someone in the middle whom she could not see. She cautiously approached the doors from the side and tried to see without being seen, and that's when she saw that at the center of the circle was none other than her mother.

Oh no, I don't need this, she thought and tried to decide what to do. Everything in her wanted to run, but if the story was going to get out, she didn't want her mother's to dominate the truth.

She straightened her clothes and marched out with her head held high.

"Mama, we need you inside," she said as calmly as she could muster. She took her mother's arm and gently tugged her, but of course her mother was not having any of it.

"Don't you be grabbing me!" she started shouting, but she let Lisa lead her away.

Meanwhile the reporters were eager to hear from Lisa: *Have you made a decision about who will receive your kidney yet? Is it true, as your mother says, that you have disowned her and your brother? Can you confirm that you intend to save your husband's life over your own brother's? Did you pull a gun on your own brother?*

Lisa kept pulling her mother toward the doors, trying to gather her thoughts. Before they went inside she paused, turned to the cameras, and said, "Look, I did not ask for this situation, and I did not ask for all these cameras and all you all getting involved in a *family concern. I* don't know what I'm going to do. *I* don't know how to make this decision. I care about everyone involved, and I need to think long and hard about what's the right thing. I would ask you all to please leave us be in the meantime."

She brought her mother inside and the reporters did not follow. She found an empty waiting room down a short hallway and led her mother to an armchair.

"What you need me for?" said Joyce.

"I don't know if 'need' is the right word," Lisa snapped back. She paced in front of her mother. "Mama, why you talk to those reporters out there?"

"Oh, you mind your own business," Joyce waved her off.

"This is *our* business, and it's about to become the whole city's dinner table conversation."

"What's so bad about that? This is a serious issue."

"You bad-mouthed me to those people and you know it."

"I told them the truth is all. I can't help if you don't come in a pretty light when you go turning your back on your own flesh and blood what is thicker than water and all. You have to live with the consequences of your actions."

"I been living with the consequences of your and T's actions, too, and I'm about tired of it, I'll tell you what."

"*My* actions? My actions was always to take care of you children, but you was always too high to 'preciate."

Lisa fell into the chair beside her mother and dropped her head on the back. She closed her eyes and let a tired, old sigh escape her.

"Mama," she said, taking as gentle a tone as she could, "don't you just get tired of all this sometimes?"

Lisa could not see the way her mother's face scowled and prepared to attack but then froze and slowly softened. When her mother spoke again, it was in a quiet tone Lisa had never heard before.

"Baby, I been tired just about all my life."

Lisa raised her head and thought for a moment.

"What I ever do to you, Mama?" she finally said.

"To *me*? Wasn't nothing you done to me, it was what you done to yourself. That frizzy hair, those frumpy clothes. You coulda been so beautiful."

Lisa fought the tears, fought to protect the wound that her mother could still inflame after all these years.

"I *am* beautiful, Mama," she stammered out. "I had to work to see it. It took work and good friends like Mila, but I finally saw it. Seems you're the only person I know who doesn't. But I am a beautiful black woman."

"Don't do you no good in this world to be a beautiful black woman. You so fair and all, you could have been more, so much more."

Her mother's voice struck her as strangely wistful, even gentle, and Lisa found herself wanting to reach out to her.

"What…what do you mean by that?" Lisa asked.

Joyce took a long time to reply, and when she did it was in the tone of one confiding in a peer, as though suddenly, or all along, she saw Lisa as an equal or partner.

"There's things I never told you, baby," she began at last, "about me. About where you come from. Time was I used to pass as one of the white folk—you know that? Back in my day, warn't too many white boys would want to take up with no black girls, but I learned to talk proper and to like the kinds of things they liked. I used to study movie posters outside the theater so I could pretend I had seen them when the kids talked about them. If they didn't know no better, well…they were as pleased to be with you as with any other girl.

"You don't remember my mama. She died when you were just a baby. I wasn't no closer to her than you were to me, though, for all that. She were dark. Really dark. You'd never peg us as related if you saw us together, and sometimes folks didn't, thought she was my nanny or something.

"All her days she worked cleaning rich white folks' houses. She brought me, sometimes, until I got old enough so's I couldn't take it anymore. The way she'd 'Yes'm' and 'No'm' those people. Not that I can say they wasn't nice to her, but I couldn't stand her being so meek and mild with them—my own mama!

"Your daddy was just a boy. His family was gonna pay for me to get rid of you until they found out who I really was. Then they just acted like I didn't exist. What was I going to do? I couldn't do nothing.

"I hated him and I hated them and I hated my mama. I guess I was pretty bitter about you, too, having to raise a little girl all on my own like that. I left you with my mama and got a job as a secretary to earn some money. He took to me, all right. Didn't even mind that I had a baby at home. He used to come onto me right there in the office, with the door closed. He sure was surprised when Terrance came along with his chestnut-brown skin. He tried to fire me, but I told him I'd bring my baby around to see his wife sometime. I did it, anyway, a few months later. That's how deep my hate went. I'd planned it all along. I seduced a man and ruined his marriage just to punish him for being white."

"Mama," Lisa said. "I had no idea. You always been so proud of being black."

"With you it didn't matter, but Terrance was so dark...I needed to protect my little boy. I blamed myself for his color, that's the truth. I thought, 'Here's a boy who's gonna get kicked and spit on all his life like his grandmama, and it's all a'cause I'm his mama.' But you... you, I thought, could rise above it. You could get what I couldn't. But you didn't want any of that. Never did.

"And the craziness of it all is that somehow you got it now without even trying. You got it and you don't hardly appreciate it. And I...I don't know if I'm angrier that you left us or that you didn't get far enough away. And now Terrance is in trouble, and I can't help him. I can't help my baby boy. I'm just...so tired, Lisa..."

Lisa cautiously scooted herself closer to her mother, who was resting her head in her hands. She put a hand on her shoulder and just sat there with her while her mother breathed deep, sad breaths.

After a while, she said, "Thank you for telling me that, Mama."

Joyce suddenly recoiled under her touch and grunted like she'd been burned then stood up and scurried away.

27

The Children

Yolanda took a couple days after her release from the hospital to spend some time at her aunt's place in Indiana with her father and kids. Terrance was eventually released from the hospital into the custody of the police. Lisa and Paul went back to work, back to the long, stressful hours. Their companies said they understood and to take as much time as they needed, but they each knew that underneath the official compassion was the expectation that "as much time as they needed" should not be very much time at all.

"You need to save up your leave time for the surgery," Lisa told her husband. It wasn't a decision so much as a practical consideration. If she ultimately chose him, they should be ready.

Meanwhile, Lisa and Jazmin were the new darlings of the agency. They were given a new account that also had a racial dimension, and Dean said some vague things about the agency trying to build a reputation for working with multicultural audiences. But that didn't mean a promotion or a raise yet, just more work for both of them.

A week earlier, she would have been excited at the prospect of making her mark and moving up in the company, but what a week it had been. There was one particular conversation that had begun to change Lisa's life more than anything ever had before.

She had called Yolanda a couple days after she'd taken the kids to Indiana.

"How are things, sweetie?" she asked.

"Michael still won't say nothing or do much of anything," was the report, "but at least we all safe."

"Yeah, that's the important thing, isn't it?"

"My dad and I can't miss any more work, though, and I don't know what to do with the kids. I'ma have to take extra shifts to pay for the hospital bills as it is, and my dad can't handle the baby right now. My aunt says leave 'em with her, which maybe I should, even if I never get to see 'em for a time."

"What about school?"

"I don't know. I don't know." Yolanda broke down crying. "How'm I s'posed to do this? How's anyone s'posed to figure this out?"

Later that night she met Paul as he came in the door.

"Paul, I need to tell you something. Don't be mad."

"What is it, babe?"

"I told Yolanda she and the kids could move in with us. Might be for a few months, until she gets her feet under her after the hospital stay."

Lisa could see Paul wanting to be noble and generous and act like this was the most obvious thing in the world, but he was also wrestling with the surprise of it all.

"It's okay, isn't it, baby?" she asked.

"Well, yeah, I mean…You just never took this much interest in your family before."

"Well, it is what it is. I just couldn't see her leaving them hours away with her aunt while she worked all the time all on her own."

"No, you're right. It'll be a bit of a change, won't it? But it's a good thing to do."

The more he thought about it the more he smiled, and she knew it was the thought of having kids in the house, and she was glad to be able to give him that, even for just a little while.

Lisa had never imagined what difference children would make. That is, she had imagined the mess and the noise and the feeling that her time and space were no longer her own to do with as she pleased, but she had not understood that, even though at times it would drive her crazy, she would come to enjoy it, to love it, even. Within a couple days she forgot that they were bound to leave in the future.

Tommy would run around the house holding Tammy and make her interact with everyone as if she were a puppet. Sometimes Tommy would save his homework until Paul came home, and Lisa would hear them at the dining room table working through math problems and practicing reading aloud.

She learned to change Tammy's diaper, which was not a skill she'd ever wanted to learn, but she came to enjoy the quiet face-to-face time with her little niece. It was like a little game to keep all her little scrambling limbs out of the way while cleaning up the mess and slipping the clean diaper in place. She learned how to gently grab little waving ankles and to keep up a constant flow of bubbly baby talk. And the best part was gathering the little thing up in her arms and hugging her to her chest, feeling that warmth and delicacy and spiraling energy all at once.

This new normal wasn't exactly free and easy, of course. Besides the constant question hanging over Lisa's head, Michael still wasn't speaking, which was a source of deep grief for Yolanda. Paul and Lisa paid for him to see a therapist, who played games with him and had him draw pictures and told them not to pressure him to speak, to let him come out of it on his own. Daisy took care of the baby during the day for much less than a day care would have cost, and though they didn't need the help, Yolanda's dad insisted on contributing from his own meager resources.

After a couple more weeks Terrance was tried and convicted for domestic battery. He was sentenced to five months less time served. Per the doctor's recommendations, he was kept on strict medical observation and given a barrage of medications. The doctor thought he had three-to-five months, max, before total, lethal kidney failure.

That was less time than they gave Paul, and Paul began to lose energy, to lose weight but also swell up at times, to generally look sickly. His firm allowed him to work a quarter, then nearly half time from home, and gave him no new clients for the time being, but it was difficult for him to keep up with the work he had.

Lisa would run into her mother once in a while when she went to see Terrance on Saturday mornings. These visits surprised everyone, but she only shrugged and said it seemed the right thing to do.

In fact, it was a kind of research, though she would not have been able to put it that way. It was research into her own feelings, her motivations. It was field work into this unknown, impossible territory where she was both the most and least powerful person.

She and Terrance didn't talk about the kidney or the attack or anything much, just what had gone on that week, however insignificant. She told him how her colleague Jazmin had saved her butt by picking up the slack on their project during those first few days, and how now they are working on the next phase, which would give them a lot more visibility within the company if all goes well. He told her how the hot water had been broken for three days, how the Salisbury steak was actually all right.

She took little away from these meetings, and she couldn't have told anyone how they were impacting her thinking on what she would do. Terrance never asked, anyway. Neither did Paul. Mila, Veronica, and Jason would ask, their heads leaning over in deep sympathy. She loved them for caring, but they didn't really know how to help, and sometimes being with them, feeling the constant presence of her problem hovering among them, was so intolerable she just had to leave.

And her mother. Her mother she avoided more than ever because she was more oppressive than ever. Making herself vulnerable to her daughter had only inflamed Joyce's self-hatred, which made her dig deeper into her ingrained habits of manipulation and abuse. There were phone calls, drop-ins, and hand-written notes in the mail. An unceasing cacophony of pleading, cajoling, accusing, sweet-talking, and whatever other desperate means Joyce laid hold of at the time.

Rick was suddenly over at the house a lot. He took a surprising interest in the children and in Terrance's recovery. He was very solicitous of Yolanda, offering to pick up things from the store for her or to take them places. He gave Lisa many occasions to raise her eyebrows in her husband's direction, though Paul stubbornly refused to get involved, and he'd later insist that Rick was harmless and there was nothing to worry about.

"Nothing to worry about?" Lisa cried on one of these occasions. "He all but felt her up right in front of us!"

"He was just hugging her! He always hugs her before he goes home. Besides, Yolanda doesn't seem to mind the attention…"

"I hope you're not insinuating what I *think* you're insinuating," Lisa warned.

"I'm not insinuating," said Paul. "I'm saying outright: Rick wouldn't do nothing if he wasn't getting signals."

"I thought you said he wasn't doing nothing anyhow?"

"I said he was harmless. I'm not stupid. I see what's going on. It's you who's not seeing it because you don't trust Rick."

"I trust him to have *our* backs, but I don't trust him to respect Terrance, none. A man goes to prison for a couple months and it means another man can move in on his wife?"

"All I'm saying is that Rick wouldn't enter if someone hadn't opened the door to him."

"I wish I could believe that."

28

Conversations II

"T, tell me it'll be different when you get out of here," Lisa said. Terrance looked at her from behind the glass and shrugged.

"You know how it is, Lise," he said into the phone. "Only one way out of the life."

"Bull crap. I got out. You never tried to get out."

"It's different for girls. You know that. I was a goner by the time I was nine or ten, yo. This is me, Lise. This the hand life dealt me. I done what I could with it, but I guess I got screwed in the end."

"Don't say that. It ain't over yet."

"That's for you to decide, big sis."

"Tell me about my boys."

"Don't Yolanda come here ever?"

"You know she don't."

"But I'm sure your other ladies all come by to make sure you're all right."

"Come on, Lisa. Now you're just being cruel. I never claimed to be perfect."

"Oh, no, you never claimed to be perfect. You just always prance around saying how you're right about this and so-and-so is wrong about that and ain't ever'body treating you so badly all the time and all that."

"Come on tell me about my kids, Sa-sa."

"They kids. You know. They bounce back pretty quick. Paul been helping Tommy with his schoolwork. Tammy's a real sweetie, I'll give you that."

"Michael start talking yet?"

"No, not yet. But I've seen him smile a couple times when Tommy and Tammy were playing together. I think he's coming out of it slowly."

"Poor kid. I never got to tell him I was sorry."

"I never heard you say before that you were."

"I…I done some bad things…to those kids. Things I am not proud of. It took sitting in here staring at a concrete wall to realize it."

"The system works."

"It's working for me, I guess."

"I been thinking about Mr. White. You remember Mr. White, T?"

"The big dude always took us to church? Oh, yeah."

"I always liked him."

"Me, too, even though I didn't much care for church."

"Oh, no? I liked that, too."

"I liked getting out of the house, and that big blue car of his, and how he'd buy us candy."

"He always had a kind word for us. I used to wish he was our dad, so he coulda always been around to say nice things to us."

"Yeah, well, Mama didn't want nothing to do with him."

"I never did know why."

"Mama been by the other day."

"Oh, yeah?"

"It ain't easy for her to come up here. She gotta take, like, three buses. Take about all day."

"Uh-huh."

"She blaming Michael now for me being here. Says it woulda blowed over if they'd been no shooting."

"Michael was defending his mother."

"Yeah, I know. That's what I told her too."

"He never shoulda been put in that situation."

"You don't got to tell me none."

"That's good to hear, at least."

"Don't be like that, sis. I been real with you since I been locked up."

"Yeah, well I'm still mad at you."

"Fair enough. But Mama got me thinking. I want to change. If I ever get the chance, that is."

"Yeah? How's that?"

"Do right by my babies. Do right by Yolanda."

"No more drugs?"

"No more using, anyway. But a man's got to make a living."

"No more stepping out then?"

"That's right. I been thinking a lot about all that. That's all over now."

"How could you do that to your own wife in the first place?"

"You want the truth?"

"What's that?"

"Well, uh...I think I was afraid of her."

"Of Yolanda? Your own wife?"

"Yeah. Uh,...her and the kids, y'know? The responsibility. I was afraid I didn't measure up."

"You broke that poor girl's heart, you know that? What, are you crying?"

"I done so many bad things, Lise. So many things. Can you tell Yolanda I'm sorry?"

"Yeah, all right."

"Tell her she don't have to do nothing. Tell her I'll show her. I'll wait till she axe me back. I'd sure love to see those kids, though."

"So, uh, Paul..."

"It's okay, Rick, you can ask."

"We don't have to if you don't want to."

"No, I get it. I mean, it's just all anyone wants to talk about."

"Don't you?"

"Not with everyone and their grandmother, no."

"Okay then."

"What am I supposed to tell them?"

"Step off?"

"Yeah, that'll play well on the evening news."

"If only your mother-in-law could keep her mouth shut."

"She has to be in control of everything, you know? Which for her means making chaos of everyone else's life."

"Look, you don't gotta tell me stuff, but I want you to know I'm here for you."

"I know."

"I'm...I'm worried about you, man. You're in bad shape."

"True dat."

"But can I tell you something?"

"Of course, man."

"I don't honestly know what the right thing is here. I think I'm supposed to tell her to choose her brother, but I'm so fed up with that guy. I don't want him to die, or anything, but...well, it somehow doesn't feel right that I've worked so hard to make something of my life and that drug-dealing, junkie screw-up might be the one who lives through all this."

"Can't blame you for that."

"You can't tell anyone any of this, of course. It's not how we're supposed to talk, you know?"

"No, I know. But it's real, though."

"And the worst of it is that the only reason I can think for asking her to choose me is that I don't want to die."

"C'mon, Paul. Not this again."

"I'm not man enough for her, simple as that—"

"Bull crap."

"And then I screw everything up by going after Terrance. I put myself between her and her own blood. Who's she supposed to side with in that scenario?"

"With the man who chose her and actually treats her halfway decently."

"Family's family."

"If it was you having to choose between her and your sister, say...?"

"That's not fair."

"Neither is this."

"Ms. McNight, on the night of the incident, were any other persons in the house besides you, your husband, and your children?"

"No, Detective, why?"

"Did you see anyone else that night prior to meeting Rick Barone...where was it, down the street?"

"I called Rick from my father's house."

"You're sure about that?"

"Uh, yes. Yes, of course."

"And you called Mr. Barone because he was a close friend of yours."

"Well, no, not exactly. I was confused...and scared. I wasn't sure what to do. My daddy doesn't have a car. I didn't want to call 911 and pay for an ambulance. Rick was...uh...someone I knew would come if I called."

"What was your relationship with Mr. Barone like previous to that night?"

"Relationship? Well, uh, it wasn't exactly a friendship. He used to be a cop in our neighborhood. That's how I met him. Then, I don't know. I'd see him around once in a while, and he'd always say hi to me. When he turned PI he gave me his card and said to call him if I ever had any trouble."

"He have a thing for you?"

"Well, yes, I believe so. But he never acted on it. He wasn't like that."

"So he never fought with your husband or came on to you when no one was looking?"

"No, sir."

"So, Mr. Barone, a man you knew from when he was a cop but hardly talked to, dropped everything to come get you and drive you and your children to the hospital at one in the morning?"

"Yes, sir. For which I'm very grateful to him. Why are you axing me these questions?"

"Ms. McNight, I want you to know that there are some irregularities with this case that could indicate your son did *not*, in fact, shoot his father."

"Irregularities?"

"They're minor, I'll grant, but we need to take them seriously. To begin with, Michael's hands did not have as much residue as we'd expect for having fired a gun. And secondly, only his right hand had any signs of residue, which is not what we'd expect if a child shot a gun, since he'd probably use both hands to hold it."

"I see. But wait, you mean that *Rick did*? No, no, he wasn't even there. I woulda seen him."

"I'm afraid we don't have enough evidence to act on if you or someone else cannot place Mr. Barone nearer to the scene that evening. Frankly, I'm inclined, all things considered, to consider it a justifiable shooting, meaning he may not face any punishment for it."

"I appreciate your saying it may not have been Michael, Det. Kaminsky, but I don't think it was Rick neither."

"Very well, Ms. McNight. Good evening."

"Hello?"

"Hi, Yolanda. This is Rick."

"Rick? The detective was just here axing about you."

"I kinda figured. That's why I called. You okay?"

"Well he was saying maybe it wasn't Michael who shot Terrance."

"Oh, yeah? Then who'd he think it was?"

"You."

"Oh. Man. So what'd *you* say?"

"I said you wasn't there. I said I called you from my daddy's house."

"Okay, that's fine, that's fine. You sure you're all right?"

"You tell me. Is everything all right? Is there anything I should be axing you?"

"I think everything will be all right. Look, Yolanda, I think you know by now that I care about you. And I don't want to lie to you, so if you want to ask me anything, go ahead…"

186

"No. No, I don't think so. Whoever did it, though, if it wasn't Michael, I don't blame him one second. You...you know what I'm saying?"

"Okay."

"Okay."

"Good morning, Dean."

"Uh, yeah, hi, good morning, Lisa."

"Can I do something for you? Are you going to introduce me to these guys?"

"They're with our HR contractor..."

"They're...what do you mean?"

"Lisa, look—"

"What's going on, Dean? Why are you acting so funny?"

"You know I like you, think you're a great person. We all do. But lately, you've been a bit...unpredictable."

"No. Dean, no. Don't do this. You know I got medical problems with my family. You can't fire me over medical problems. I do good work for you."

"Yeah, well, that's the thing. It's come to our attention that Jazmin has been doing the bulk of your good work—"

"Jazmin? She tells you that? Wait, there she is, she'll tell you— Jazmin! Jazmin! Hold up!"

"Lisa, leave her alone..."

"Jazmin, where are you going? Come back. Hey, get your hands off me!"

"I'm sorry, Lisa, but we can't let you harass Ms. Darwish."

"Harass?"

"Ms. Darwish has expressed concern that you have told her stories of you and your family getting violent as recently as the last couple months. She says she's afraid if she stands up to you, you might..."

"Might what? Might *what*? Dean, you know me! You know this isn't right! That witch sold me out!"

"Lisa, I'm sorry. It's out of my hands. The partners are worried that the things going on in your family life may reflect badly on the agency. There's nothing I can do."

"Dean…"

"I think it's best if you gather your things. These gentlemen will see you out of the building."

"Dean…"

"I'm sorry, Lisa."

"But…"

"I want to thank you so much for taking me and the kids these last few weeks. We'll be out of your hair, soon, I promise."

"Girl, you don't have to thank me all the time. It's been our pleasure, really. I'm just sorry I didn't get to know the kids sooner. They're really great. And Paul loves kids."

"They can be such a handful, sometimes I forget how great they are."

"It's been good for Paul and me to have them around. It's good to have a kind of project or, you know, responsibility right now."

"Michael really looks up to Paul."

"You think so? I thought he and Tommy were getting on better."

"Tommy likes Paul, but he's loyal to his dad, you know? But Michael be watching everything Paul does. Lord knows he's a better role model than T has been."

"I don't want to say nothing about that. My feelings about my brother have always been…complicated."

"Yeah, mine too."

"I…I know we were never close, but…how come you let him treat you the way he do—if I can ask?"

"He charmed me with that big smile of his, I guess."

"Some things a smile can't cover up."

"We can't all find a Paul, you know. They's slim pickin's in the hood. You get a guy who makes you feel even a little bit special, buys you nice things, says he wants you to have his babies…. It's hard to leave that on the table when the alternative is to be all alone. He almost never hit me before that night, and never with a weapon."

"Honey, I ain't judging, but the great tragedy of the black woman is she don't expect more from her man than a baby, some beans in the pantry, and only hitting her a couple times a month."

"The great tragedy of the black woman is the black man. You try to make him treat you right and he run off to find some white witch who got some screwed up fantasies about dark men pushing her around."

"You might be right, there. And the tragedy of the black man is he could have any black woman he wanted if he just treated her right."

"What about the white man? You married to one."

"The tragedy of the white man? That he don't know how much he need the black woman."

"Well, Paul need you about now, I guess."

"Seem like about everybody need me now."

"Dear God, you know I don't pray enough, but I suppose you don't care about any of that. I know you're a god who celebrates when the prodigal son come home, so here's your prodigal daughter standing at the gate. Help me. Help me make this decision. Let it be the right one. I don't want to lose anyone. I don't know how to decide who lives and who dies. Is this what it's like being you? Or is it what it's like to be human? May Paul forgive me for my weakness, for drawing this out, for not loving him like I should. But Lord, I can't…I can't do this."

29

Lisa's Choice Is Made

After only five weeks in prison, Terrance had been sent back to the hospital for a kidney infection, and the doctor said he would need to be monitored for several days before he could be released.

Lisa slept at home Wednesday night so she could get some decent sleep and take a shower. It felt good to be in her own bed after so many nights on the convertible chair in the hospital, though with Paul gone she was haunted by thoughts of his absence becoming permanent.

She spent a long time letting the steam of the shower work its way into her shoulders and neck, trying to forget that anything existed beyond the mist and the mosaic-blue patterns of the tile and shower curtain. But every now and then she could hear Yolanda raising her voice at the children as she hurried them out the door to school. It was still another day. Her sister-in-law, nephews, and niece were still in her home, her husband and brother were still in the hospital. And she still did not know what she would do.

The sadness welled up from her chest and pressed from behind her face. *Just one tear*, she thought. *If I could cry just one tear*...But the mere thought of permitting herself to feel the sadness was enough to break open the gates and let it burst forth, and she leaned her head against the tile, still cool against the outside wall, and thought *Why? Why? Why, God, is this happening to me? Please help me!*

She did manage to sleep in a little, despite the children's noise, and as she descended the stairs she caught the warming, roasted smell of coffee.

"Oh, Daisy, you're my angel!" she said as she entered the kitchen and inhaled deeply. Daisy handed her a hot cup.

"Good morning. I figured you might like your coffee ready for you since you slept in so late."

"It's perfect, thank you."

Lisa sat down and asked Daisy to turn on the small TV that faced the breakfast table from the counter. The news was entering its last segment, and Jill Robinson looked at the camera with her big brown eyes and red silk scarf and said, "And now an update on a story about a south side woman facing an impossible choice. Lisa Drayton's husband and brother are both in need of a kidney transplant, and Ms. Drayton is a donor match for both of them."

Daisy gave Lisa a worried look. Lisa sighed and said, "It's okay. They were outside the hospital last night, but I slipped out a different exit."

Jill Robinson was saying, "News 2 has learned that as of early this week, the situation has become more dire. Ms. Drayton's brother, Terrance McNight, serving a domestic battery conviction, was transferred last weekend to St. Anne's Hospital due to complications related to kidney failure. Then on Monday, Paul Drayton, husband to Ms. Drayton, was also admitted to St. Anne's for similar reasons. Ms. Joyce McNight, mother to Lisa and Terrance, reports that both men are now in immediate need of a kidney transplant. Ms. McNight also reports that Ms. Drayton, who had at one time planned to donate her kidney to her husband, has now decided to give it to her brother..."

"Oh my goodness, please change this," Lisa said. Daisy changed the channel. *Jenny Jones* was on, but it was even worse than the news, for her guest was none other than Joyce.

"It's terrible, Jenny," Joyce was saying. "My poor boy all laid up in the hospital like that, and with three kids to feed at home."

"I can't believe this," Lisa said, justifying herself to Daisy. "I told her not to talk to any of these people!"

Jenny Jones said to Joyce, "Illness in the family is always diffi-cult, but what makes this story particularly compelling and challeng-ing is that your daughter is a donor match for her brother, but her husband is in the hospital at the same time, also needing a kidney transplant, and she's a match for him, too. Now, I understand that because her husband's illness came to light earlier, your daughter, Lisa, had originally intended to donate a kidney to him…"

"That's right, Jenny. She always did think of others. But when her brother got sick, she knew she'd have to do the right thing and give the kidney to him."

Lisa's stomach about turned over. Jenny Jones sat in an armchair near her mother and leaned in close to take her hand.

"Your daughter didn't want to come on the show to talk about this, and we want to be sensitive to how hard this must be on her, but what do you think she would want us to know if she were here?"

"She'd say they's nothing more important than flesh and blood. You can't help everybody you want to help, you know? So you got to choose who's most important, and that's family."

"Daisy, I'm going to take this coffee to go," Lisa said. "I need to get to the hospital."

She rushed to Paul's room and was relieved to see he wasn't watching the TV. In fact, he'd slept until recently. She told him what her mother had and done.

"But don't worry, honey, I haven't made any decision yet. I don't want anyone upsetting you because they saw her say those things."

"It's all right, babe. I know you'll tell me first once you've made up your mind."

He lay there so pale and green and sickly but still smiling at her, that smile of his that was such a comfort to her in days gone by but that now was mixed with sadness like he was already waving goodbye to her, and though she convulsed with the effort she tried to fight more tears but could not.

When she lifted her head she left a large wet tear stain on his bedsheets.

"I hate seeing you like this, babe," Paul said. "No one should have to make this choice, least of all someone as good and kind as you."

"I'll be all right," Lisa said weakly.

"Hand me that paper over there."

"This one?"

"Yeah." Paul unfolded the paper. "I wrote this the other night before your big meeting but didn't have a chance to share it. Then you got fired, and it didn't feel right. But I think now's as good a time as any."

"Oh, Paul."

"Don't start with the crying again or I won't be able to read it.

"There is no memory of this, of us,
here, entwined in a tangled hope, of these
anxious breaths. Nor is there the arching,
fearful entropy awaiting us.

Just the freshest joy of now, only now.
No glancing far behind, no
recollections bittersweet of lost
loves or discarded desire.

For you, a new leaf of an eternal today
For me, a twig of sweet
Happenstance from the tree of errant dreams
giving you, and me, and this short life,
a chance."

"I'ma have to read it again later, but I know I loved it," Lisa said.

"Lisa, it's okay. I've decided to make the decision for you. It's the only way. It's got to be Terrance."

He had caught her off guard, and she needed a second to process.

"No, Paul…"

"It's okay, I promise. You already showed me how much you loved me when you volunteered before all this stuff with Terrance.

That itself was everything to me. I don't need anything else. We had a good life together. It wasn't always perfect, but I know I've been a lucky man. Maybe Terrance can turn his life around if he gets this second chance. I've lived the life I wanted to live."

"Paul, honey, you're really amazing, you know that? But how could I live without you?"

"You never needed me as much as I needed you. I think we both know that."

"It's not true. It's not. I needed your strength, your goodness. I wanted to get as far from my old life as I could, but with every other guy I was always afraid he would find out and it would be over. But you knew me in that old life and you still loved me. That was *my* everything."

Lisa crawled onto the bed with him and snuggled up under his arm, laughing and crying and generally feeling a mess. Everything and everybody was pushing her toward Terrance, but she still couldn't make the choice herself. It was as if chains had been thrown around her and she were being dragged toward an inevitability, and maybe it would be easier if she walked of her own accord, but the very fact of the chains made her resist and told her something was wrong. Even as Paul spoke she realized his permission or encouragement was not enough. She needed to choose for her own reasons, if she could only find out what they were.

They lay for a long time until Paul drifted off to sleep again. Then she went down the hall to Terrance's room.

"Did you know about this *Jenny Jones* crap?" she asked when she saw he was awake.

He grimaced and shrugged his shoulders. "Yeah, she told me yesterday she was gonna do it. I just watched it…"

"And why didn't you tell me? Or try to stop her?"

"Who says I didn't? What am I supposed to do, hold her down? She wouldn't let me tell you cuz she said you had your chance and this was hers. Look, don't pay her no mind, all right?"

"Don't pay her no mind? She's blabbing our business all over the city! I have to live in this town."

"You know how she be. But I know this between you and me, yo? I know I'ma be the first to know when you come to a decision."

"I can't keep doing this, T. I can't." Lisa fell into a chair in the far corner. The tears came again, and she put her head in her hands.

"She really getting to you, ain't she?" Terrance said.

"Yeah, she is."

"Everything always seemed to roll off your back," he continued. "I didn't know it hit you so hard."

"A week from today either my brother or my husband will likely be dead, and my own mother is making a fool of herself on the television making up stories to suit her own twisted view of reality. Yeah, it hits me hard."

The morning sun shone directly on her chair and warmed her all over. They sat quietly, and she allowed the sunlight to slowly sedate her until she actually dozed off into a light sleep.

It was not long after this that Joyce rushed into the room. Noticing her daughter in the corner, she stopped short, but when she saw Lisa was asleep her excitement immediately returned.

"Did you see? Did you see?" she said.

"Yeah, I saw," Terrance answered.

"It's all gonna be all right, I know it is, baby."

"Mama, come sit down," Terrance said, and the sudden stillness in his voice took her out of her reverie. She sat next to his bed, facing him.

"What is it, baby?"

"You always so hard on Lisa."

"Huh? Why you say that?"

"Because it's true. And because this is a hard thing for her. She could use your support."

"Yes, okay, T. I suppose so. But it's tough raising a girl, you know."

"Nah, but it wasn't like that, was it? You always treated me better. I was always the wonder child in your eyes, even though she was the one with all the accomplishments."

"It wasn't about the accomplishments, Terrance. I love you, baby."

"I know, Mama, but tell me. Lisa has to decide between two men she cares about, which one will live and which one will die. Tell me why you was always so hard on her. What she ever do to you?"

Lisa had awoken and raised her head. Their mother did not notice she was awake because her back was to her daughter, but Terrance locked eyes with his sister and in his look she understood that she should be still and quiet.

"T, if I tell you something, you have to promise never to tell another soul, you hear?" Joyce said.

"Okay, Mama."

"I don't know how to say it, but maybe I really am jealous of Lisa, and it always just killed me inside to feel that way."

"But why, Mama?"

"Well, okay...I guess I'll tell you."

Lisa expected to hear a reprise of what her mother had told her earlier, but instead it was even more of the story.

"My father was white, you know that? My mama worked as a maid for a big rich white family in Alabama. Lived in the attic of they mansion. The master there, he snuck around with my mama, just like in old plantation days, just exactly like it was old plantation days, dammit. She loved him till her dying breath, but he didn't do no more than to keep paying her wages and letting her bastard child live with her and then send me to some decent schools.

"And because I saw the way my mama loved the master of that house, I thought he must be as good a man as she thought him. I thought having what those folks had was about the best life you could ask for. And look at me! I'm hardly more browner than the inside of an acorn. I just about could pass at school and in the neighborhood, but when my mama was walking by my side, well everyone knew I was just as much a colored person as she was.

"Now, don't interrupt me, son. I know exactly what I'm saying. Your sister never did understand what she could have had. She could have marched through this world with every privilege and advantage of a white woman all the while holding within her the strength and spirit of our African ancestors. She could have just about had it all, but wouldn't she just do everything she could to look as frumpy and nerdy and *black* as she could be?

"And then, you know what? She goes and finds herself a white lawyer and she gets it all. *As a black woman.* And she hardly give us the time of day. Now how'm I supposed to feel, when I couldn't make it nowhere, myself, as either a white woman or a black woman?

"So that, I suppose, now's I think about it, is why I was always so hard on her. Some piece of crap mama you have, huh? That make you happy to know that?"

Terrance was breathing heavily, but he had listened intently. He saw the silent tears streaming down Lisa's face. Lisa wanted to hear the story yet again, to see if another layer would be revealed, to see if, through the telling, another chink in her mother's armor might fall away, but she remembered the way her mother had flinched under her touch not long ago.

"It's not her fault, Mama," Terrance said.

"Ain't about whose fault it is. S'about what's right and what's wrong, and she done treated us wrong."

"We treated her wrong her whole life, I guess."

"I tried to show her," Joyce mumbled. "I didn't know how to make her do it…"

"A kind word, Mama," came Lisa's voice from behind her. "It's all I ever wanted."

Joyce jumped up and spun around, a look as of a trapped rat in her eyes. Lisa saw suddenly, through the lens of her mother's past, a woman who had spent her whole life defending herself, justifying herself, protecting her heart from all the people who kept proving to her that she deserved to be trampled upon. Probably she'd never bared her soul to anyone like she had to Terrance, or at least not since Lisa's father, and now she felt the old feeling of injury and attack.

But what could a daughter do? As much as she felt compassion rising within her, Lisa's wounds were just as deep as her mother's, and they were wounds her mother created. How could she offer comfort when her own heart was cringing in pain?

It was too late, anyway. The animal was loose. Joyce's eyes flamed and she went on the attack.

"You was listenin' to me this whole time? You eavesdropping on you own mama now?"

"No, Mama—" Lisa pleaded.

"You enjoy hearing about your mama's mixed up life? You holding it over me now?"

"Mama, please, no—"

"You nosy crazy, self-important, freaking-ugly witch!" Joyce shrieked.

"Mama, please, stop!" Lisa cried. She rose and took a conciliatory step forward, reaching out pleading arms.

"You always thought you was better than us! You always holding it over us! You think you can do whatever you want, and now you gone let my baby boy die cuz you got yourself a rich white man to take care of!"

"Mama, please, I'm scared!"

"Oh, now you scared! Poor little rich lady is scared her ghetto mama gonna giver her what's coming to her!"

"No, Mama, that's not...I'm not..."

"Then what? What? What you of all people got to be scared of?"

Lisa wasn't sure exactly, herself, just what she was afraid of, and her mother wasn't about to give her a chance to say it. She just kept barraging her with insults and accusations.

"I'm scared...I'm scared..." Lisa kept saying through convulsive sobs.

Her daughter's vulnerability only enraged Joyce all the more, and she charged her and began to slap her and beat her as she cowered away against the window.

Her mother wasn't strong enough to physicaly hurt her, but the blows hit raw interior wounds. She heard Terrance shouting now, though she couldn't understand what. She just kept repeating, "I'm scared, I'm scared."

Suddenly she shoved her mother away from her with an explosive gesture. Joyce fell against Terrance's bed and then onto her knees. She immediately began to raise herself, but it gave Lisa time to say what she did not know she had needed to say. She just opened her mouth and shouted, and what she heard herself saying was, "I'm scared I'll let my husband die and you *still* won't love me, Mama!"

It was like Joyce comprehended nothing, or rather, the emotional pathways of her mind were so twisted that she heard something no one else heard in her daughter's words. What she heard was not deep-seated trauma and pain but accusation and judgment.

"That's right!" she screamed. "I'll *never* love you! You slut! You freaking—"

She had started to charge her daughter again, but something jerked her back. It was Terrance. He had quickly reached out and grabbed her arm, and though his strength was not what it used to be, he found the inner resources to grip her firmly and pull her back to the bed.

"What is it, baby, are you all right?" Joyce said, suddenly softened with the kind of concern you might expect from a mother.

"No, Mama, I ain't all right," T said. He looked her straight in the eyes. "I can't watch this anymore. You didn't hear a word Lisa just said to you. You never heard a thing she said to you. Maybe you never heard a word *I* said to you. But it ain't right, Mama. None of this. You tole me I could do no wrong, and look where it got me. You tole her she couldn't do nothing right, and she said *Freak you* and made something of herself, but all the time all either of us ever wanted was a mother. Someone to love us and teach us right from wrong so we didn't have to learn it all the hard way."

"No, Terrance, baby, no," Joyce whimpered.

"Yeah, Mama. It's all true and you know it. And the worst part is, I believed you. I believed I was a golden boy who everybody should love and who would always come out all right, and worse than that, I believed Lisa was all the things you said. No, Mama, this ain't right, and it's got to stop. You and me, we got to stop."

He winced to see the look of pain and utter confusion on his mother's face. It was as if a god was rejecting her, or rather, as if an idol was tearing itself down and revealing it was nothing but dust.

He reached out his hand to Lisa. She had been shaking her head, refusing this act, refusing to let him make the decision for her—refusing any decision at all. She stared at his hand, just his hand, held out for her. An offer. All she had to do was accept. He wasn't making the choice for her; he was offering to hold her hand while she made it for herself.

She hesitated, wondered if she had the strength, wondered if he would withdraw should she reach out, and then…she took his hand.

Tears broke from her eyes, and each tear was day and an hour of holding her world at bay with sheer force of will. She felt at once as if she'd sunken into a warm, dark sea and emerged onto a bright meadow. She felt both steady on her feet and as if she was floating above the ground. The fear, anger, hatred, self-doubt, and self-deception were burning away, and she knew she could do what she had to.

"You weren't such a bad big sister," Terrance said. "When I let you be, anyway. I'm sorry, Lisa."

"T-Thank you."

Joyce continued to stare with the look of someone for whom the earth itself had dropped out and she suddenly found herself floating in a blank nothingness, but Terrance and Lisa met each other's eyes and were crying together.

"I can't undo all the stuff we did to you, but I can try to make things right now," Terrance continued. "It's gotta be Paul, Lisa. You go help your husband. You won't be able to live with yourself any other way, and I don't want to live knowing it cost you everything like that."

"No,…no," Joyce moaned as Terrance's words made their way to her over the vast distances of her isolation.

"It's okay, Mama. It's okay, sis. I'm ready to die. I think, anyways. I know you'll look after Yolanda and the kids. I know…I know folks will probably be better without me, really…"

"No, T, don't say that, don't say that," Lisa said through her sobs.

"You should go to Paul now. You got some things to arrange. Could I…maybe I could get a hug, first?"

When was the last time she had hugged him? It could be fifteen or twenty years. She leaned over his bed and wrapped her arms around him. Then she kissed his cheek and whispered, *Thank you*. It seemed so little for what he'd just done, but it was all she had.

She stayed with Terrance and cried with him until they were both cried out. Their mother sat down and still looked shocked and never did seem to comprehend what had happened. When she had recovered her breath, Lisa rose, kissed Terrance again, and left to join her husband.

30

A Funeral

The organist filled the church with a somber hymn. People in black suits and dark dresses formed a line up to the front of the sanctuary where an elegant white casket surrounded by white and yellow and purple flowers held the earthly remains of Terrance McNight. The people filed past and then found seats in the pews.

A minister stood up, said some words about memory and love and resurrection, and the people cried and nodded. The choir stood up and sang "Going Up Yonder."

> *If anybody ask you*
> *Where I'm going*
> *Where I'm going soon*
> *I'm goin' up yonder*

A sober woman closed the coffin. Men with white gloves lifted it and carried it down the aisle to the hearse waiting outside the doors. There was a procession and an open grave and more good words about dust and ashes, and everyone put a flower on the casket and then it was lowered down into the earth.

Then everyone returned to the church basement and had ham sandwiches and potato salad and cookies. Mila, Veronica, and Jason were there, as was Steve. They hugged Lisa and cried with her and they talked quietly at their own table. Paul stayed put in a chair the whole time and ate very little, and Lisa would not leave his side.

Joyce sat at another table among a few neighbors she called friends, though they perhaps came more for the memory of the young Terrance's charm and charisma than for any loyalty to his mother.

When Joyce rose and began to walk toward Lisa, everyone seemed to see it at once. Jason leapt up and tried to intercept her, but she waved him off and said she wanted to speak with her daughter—but there was none of the usual contempt and spite, and Jason backed off.

Lisa rose so as to meet her mother face to face. Paul grabbed her hand and hoped for the best. Joyce didn't speak at first, just stood there looking in her daughter's face. It was disconcerting, that look. It was a look of someone trying to focus their blurry eyes on a thing in the distance, but a thing that they had been searching for and hoping for a long time. It brought tears to Lisa's eyes, and she needed to break the spell somehow.

"I'm sorry, Mama. I'm so sorry..." she sputtered.

Joyce stepped forward and Lisa reflexively stepped back while the rest of the room tensed up for a fight, but Joyce's arms opened and embraced her daughter, and Lisa fell completely to pieces.

"Come here, baby," Joyce said. "My poor baby girl. I ain't done right by you, I know. And look at us now. Burying Terrance who we thought would outlive all of us. How could someone with so much life ever die? How is it possible? This world all messed up, and I helped mess it up."

No one knew quite what to do. It was too shocking to be simply joyful; they were waiting to see if there wouldn't be an explosion after all.

"Terrance and I talked a lot in the last days. I didn't want to hear most of it because I didn't want to accept he was gonna die. But now he's gone, I find I can't hold onto the anger anymore. Oh, Lisa, hold onto me. I'm scared I'm like to follow after him. Oh, my baby!"

Jason came up and helped Joyce take a chair next to Lisa and they sat together holding each other and crying.

"Terrance made his peace with God, I know that," Joyce said. "He in a better place now, I do believe. I only wish it didn't take him dying for one of you to finally get through to me."

"It's okay, Mama," said Lisa.

"No, dearie, it ain't okay, but maybe I can make it a little better, by and by."

Jason, who was still standing behind Joyce, began to sing, and the song was picked up by the others in the room, and the grief-stricken, makeshift church-basement choir sang beauty and comfort and peace to one another.

> *I can take the pain*
> *The heartaches they bring*
> *The comfort in knowing*
> *I'll soon be gone*
> *As God gives me grace*
> *I'll run this race*
> *Until I see my Savior*
> *Face to face*
> *I'm goin' up yonder*
> *To be with my Lord*

About the Author

Jackie Glanton is a manager at a member-based physician organi-
zation and the author of *Blood Is Thicker Than Water*. She lives in
Chicago, Illinois, with her husband and enjoys long walks along the
lakefront and through the forest preserves, while taking in all that
Mother Nature has to offer. Jackie earned her BA in Finance from
Loyola University and her MBA from Roosevelt University. From
there, she began her career in healthcare management, and although
her work is not in direct patient care, she found herself increasingly
obsessed with helping women that were in abusive relationships by
either their partners or family members. With over a decade of men-
toring young women on physical and verbal abuse, Jackie has spent
the last couple of years developing and writing a novel depicting how
those closest to you can send you down a road of despair and hope-
lessness. Jackie has walked the paths of her characters all while still
being hunted by many challenges and hurtful memories from her
childhood and as a young adult. Trust in God and you too will over-
come any obstacles placed along your path.